SOCIETY FOR OLD TESTAMENT STUDY

MONOGRAPH SERIES

GENERAL EDITOR
R. E. CLEMENTS

4

RELICS OF ANCIENT EXEGESIS

A STUDY OF
THE MISCELLANIES IN 3 REIGNS 2

RELICS OF
ANCIENT EXEGESIS

A STUDY OF
THE MISCELLANIES IN 3 REIGNS 2

D. W. GOODING

Reader in Classics
The Queen's University of Belfast

CAMBRIDGE UNIVERSITY PRESS

CAMBRIDGE

LONDON · NEW YORK · MELBOURNE

Published by the Syndics of the Cambridge University Press
The Pitt Building, Trumpington Street, Cambridge CB2 IRP
Bentley House, 200 Euston Road, London NWI 2DB
32 East 57th Street, New York, NY 10022, USA
296 Beaconsfield Parade, Middle Park, Melbourne 3206, Australia

First published 1976

Printed in Great Britain
at the
University Printing House, Cambridge
(Euan Phillips, University Printer)

Library of Congress Cataloguing in Publication Data

Gooding, David Willoughby.

Relics of ancient exegesis.

(Monograph series – Society for Old Testament Study; 4)
Includes bibliographical references and index.
1. Bible. O.T. 1 Kings 2: 35 – Criticism, Textual.
2. Bible. O.T. 1 Kings 2: 46 – Criticism, Textual.
I. Title. II. Series: Society for Old Testament Study.
Monograph series; 4.

BS1335.2.G66   222′.53′044   74–19523
ISBN 0 521 20700 2

CONTENTS

To W. M. G.
in gratitude

PREFACE

This monograph had its first beginnings in the Grinfield Lectures on the Septuagint in the University of Oxford for 1968–9. The lectures, worked over and enlarged, were in 1971 submitted to the Society for Old Testament Study for inclusion in its monograph series. They were accepted in 1972 for publication in 1974, but unforeseen economic and organisational difficulties have delayed publication until 1976. Now that publication has at length been achieved, it renews in me most grateful memories of all those who by their friendship, hospitality, and stimulating conversation made my tenure of the Grinfield Lectureship so thoroughly enjoyable. In this connection the Revd Dr H. F. D. Sparks is especially to be thanked for his constant encouragement and the helpful criticisms and suggestions which he made after each of the lectures.

The Revd Drs J. A. Emerton and R. E. Clements have both laboured long reading the typescript and negotiating its acceptance into the Society's monograph series. For accepting the book and for their administrative labours I thank them gratefully.

I acknowledge here also my longstanding debt to Mrs Rosa Martin, Librarian of the Presbyterian College, Belfast. With her admirable grasp of the Library's rules she is never at a loss to suggest highly convenient ways of borrowing books for unconscionably long periods of time. It is right that she should be praised.

Patient colleagues, generous with their time, have toiled for me at proof-reading. I record their names with gratitude: Mr D. F. Payne, Dr R. J. A. Talbert, Dr G. J. Wenham. The officers of the Cambridge University Press with their customary expertise have not only achieved their usual standard of excellence, but have immensely lightened my task. Let them too be thanked and praised.

D. W. GOODING

The Queen's University, Belfast

PUBLISHER'S NOTE

The Publisher and author are grateful to Würtembergische Bibelanstatt, Stuttgart, for permission to reproduce the text of the miscellanies (2 Kings: 35^{a-k}, 46^{a-l}) from A. Rahlf's edition, *Septuaginta id est Vetus Testamentum Graece Juxta LXX Interpretes* (1935).

THE TEXT OF THE MISCELLANIES

MISCELLANY 1

(Rahlfs' text)

5ᵃ ³⁵ᵃΚαὶ ἔδωκεν κύριος φρόνησιν τῷ Σαλωμων καὶ σοφίαν πολλὴν σφόδρα καὶ πλάτος καρδίας ὡς ἡ ἄμμος ἡ παρὰ τὴν θάλασσαν, 5ᵇ ³⁵ᵇκαὶ ἐπληθύνθη ἡ φρόνησις Σαλωμων σφόδρα ὑπὲρ τὴν φρόνησιν πάντων ἀρχαίων υἱῶν καὶ ὑπὲρ πάντας φρονίμους Αἰγύπτου. 5ᶜ ³⁵ᶜκαὶ ἔλαβεν τὴν θυγατέρα Φαραω καὶ εἰσήγαγεν αὐτὴν εἰς τὴν πόλιν Δαυιδ ἕως συντελέσαι αὐτὸν τὸν οἶκον αὐτοῦ καὶ τὸν οἶκον κυρίου ἐν πρώτοις καὶ τὸ τεῖχος Ιερουσαλημ κυκλόθεν · ἐν ἑπτὰ ἔτεσιν 5ᵈ ἐποίησεν καὶ συνετέλεσεν. ³⁵ᵈκαὶ ἦν τῷ Σαλωμων ἑβδομήκοντα χιλιάδες αἴροντες ἄρσιν καὶ ὀγδοήκοντα χιλιάδες λατόμων ἐν τῷ 5ᵉ ὄρει. ³⁵ᵉκαὶ ἐποίησεν Σαλωμων τὴν θάλασσαν καὶ τὰ ὑποστηρίγματα καὶ τοὺς λουτῆρας τοὺς μεγάλους καὶ τοὺς στύλους καὶ τὴν 5ᶠ κρήνην τῆς αὐλῆς καὶ τὴν θάλασσαν τὴν χαλκῆν. ³⁵ᶠκαὶ ᾠκοδόμησεν τὴν ἄκραν καὶ τὰς ἐπάλξεις αὐτῆς καὶ διέκοψεν τὴν πόλιν Δαυιδ · οὕτως θυγάτηρ Φαραω ἀνέβαινεν ἐκ τῆς πόλεως Δαυιδ εἰς τὸν οἶκον αὐτῆς, ὃν ᾠκοδόμησεν αὐτῇ · τότε ᾠκοδόμησεν τὴν 5ᵍ ἄκραν. ³⁵ᵍκαὶ Σαλωμων ἀνέφερεν τρεῖς ἐν τῷ ἐνιαυτῷ ὁλοκαυτώσεις καὶ εἰρηνικὰς ἐπὶ τὸ θυσιαστήριον, ὃ ᾠκοδόμησεν τῷ κυρίῳ, 5ʰ καὶ ἐθυμία ἐνώπιον κυρίου. καὶ συνετέλεσεν τὸν οἶκον. ³⁵ʰκαὶ οὗτοι οἱ ἄρχοντες οἱ καθεσταμένοι ἐπὶ τὰ ἔργα τοῦ Σαλωμων · τρεῖς χιλιάδες καὶ ἑξακόσιοι ἐπιστάται τοῦ λαοῦ τῶν ποιούντων 5ⁱ τὰ ἔργα. ³⁵ⁱκαὶ ᾠκοδόμησεν τὴν Ασσουρ καὶ τὴν Μαγδω καὶ τὴν 5ᵏ Γαζερ καὶ τὴν Βαιθωρων τὴν ἐπάνω καὶ τὰ Βααλαθ · ³⁵ᵏπλὴν μετὰ τὸ οἰκοδομῆσαι αὐτὸν τὸν οἶκον τοῦ κυρίου καὶ τὸ τεῖχος Ιερουσαλημ κύκλῳ, μετὰ ταῦτα ᾠκοδόμησεν τὰς πόλεις ταύτας.

I

MISCELLANY 2

(Rahlfs' text)

2 : 46ᵃ ⁴⁶ᵃΚαὶ ἦν ὁ βασιλεὺς Σαλωμων φρόνιμος σφόδρα καὶ σοφός, καὶ
Ιουδα καὶ Ισραηλ πολλοὶ σφόδρα ὡς ἡ ἄμμος ἡ ἐπὶ τῆς θαλάσσης
46ᵇ εἰς πλῆθος, ἐσθίοντες καὶ πίνοντες καὶ χαίροντες· ⁴⁶ᵇκαὶ Σαλωμων
ἦν ἄρχων ἐν πάσαις ταῖς βασιλείαις, καὶ ἦσαν προσφέροντες δῶρα
καὶ ἐδούλευον τῷ Σαλωμων πάσας τὰς ἡμέρας τῆς ζωῆς αὐτοῦ.
46ᶜ ⁴⁶ᶜκαὶ Σαλωμων ἤρξατο διανοίγειν τὰ δυναστεύματα τοῦ Λιβάνου,
46ᵈ,46ᵉ ⁴⁶ᵈκαὶ αὐτὸς ᾠκοδόμησεν τὴν Θερμαι ἐν τῇ ἐρήμῳ. ⁴⁶ᵉκαὶ τοῦτο τὸ
ἄριστον τῷ Σαλωμων· τριάκοντα κόροι σεμιδάλεως καὶ ἑξήκοντα
κόροι ἀλεύρου κεκοπανισμένου, δέκα μόσχοι ἐκλεκτοὶ καὶ εἴκοσι
βόες νομάδες καὶ ἑκατὸν πρόβατα ἐκτὸς ἐλάφων καὶ δορκάδων καὶ
46ᶠ ὀρνίθων ἐκλεκτῶν νομάδων. ⁴⁶ᶠὅτι ἦν ἄρχων ἐν παντὶ πέραν τοῦ
ποταμοῦ ἀπὸ Ραφι ἕως Γάζης, ἐν πᾶσιν τοῖς βασιλεῦσιν πέραν τοῦ
46ᵍ ποταμοῦ· ⁴⁶ᵍκαὶ ἦν αὐτῷ εἰρήνη ἐκ πάντων τῶν μερῶν αὐτοῦ
κυκλόθεν, καὶ κατῴκει Ιουδα καὶ Ισραηλ πεποιθότες, ἕκαστος ὑπὸ
τὴν ἄμπελον αὐτοῦ καὶ ὑπὸ τὴν συκῆν αὐτοῦ, ἐσθίοντες καὶ
πίνοντες, ἀπὸ Δαν καὶ ἕως Βηρσαβεε πάσας τὰς ἡμέρας Σαλωμων.
46ʰ — ⁴⁶ʰκαὶ οὗτοι οἱ ἄρχοντες τοῦ Σαλωμων· Αζαριου υἱὸς Σαδωκ τοῦ
ἱερέως καὶ Ορνιου υἱὸς Ναθαν ἄρχων τῶν ἐφεστηκότων καὶ Εδραμ
ἐπὶ τὸν οἶκον αὐτοῦ καὶ Σουβα γραμματεὺς καὶ Βασα υἱὸς Αχιθαλαμ ἀναμιμνήσκων καὶ Αβι υἱὸς Ιωαβ ἀρχιστράτηγος καὶ Αχιρε
υἱὸς Εδραϊ ἐπὶ τὰς ἄρσεις καὶ Βαναια υἱὸς Ιωδαε ἐπὶ τῆς αὐλαρχίας
καὶ ἐπὶ τοῦ πλινθείου καὶ Ζαχουρ υἱὸς Ναθαν ὁ σύμβουλος. —
46ⁱ ⁴⁶ⁱκαὶ ἦσαν τῷ Σαλωμων τεσσαράκοντα χιλιάδες τοκάδες ἵπποι
46ᵏ εἰς ἅρματα καὶ δώδεκα χιλιάδες ἱππέων. ⁴⁶ᵏκαὶ ἦν ἄρχων ἐν πᾶσιν
τοῖς βασιλεῦσιν ἀπὸ τοῦ ποταμοῦ καὶ ἕως γῆς ἀλλοφύλων καὶ
ἕως ὁρίων Αἰγύπτου.
46ˡ ⁴⁶ˡΣαλωμων υἱὸς Δαυιδ ἐβασίλευσεν ἐπὶ Ισραηλ καὶ Ιουδα ἐν
Ιερουσαλημ.

2

CHAPTER I

A STRANGE PHENOMENON

In the second chapter of 3 Reigns there occurs a phenomenon which by any standard is most unusual. From the first verse of ch. 2 – indeed from the beginning of the Book – the Greek has been matching the Hebrew of the MT with a high degree of correspondence, when at the end of v. 35 suddenly and without warning the Greek diverges, and in a succession of verses, which both Brooke–McLean[1] and Rahlfs[2] number[3] 35[a]–35[o], presents material that in this position has no counterpart in the MT at all. This in itself, of course, is nothing exceptional; the Greek OT often disagrees with the MT both in order and content. The thing that makes this passage so remarkable is the nature of the material that fills vv. 35[a–k]. At first sight it looks like nothing but a collection of variant readings;[4] it is made up of the following elements:

1. Verses which word for word repeat translations which stand in the main Greek text in positions corresponding to the counterpart material in the MT. Thus, v. 35[d] repeats word for word the main Greek text at 5: 29 (BM 5: 15); at 5: 29 this material corresponds in position with its counterpart in the MT (5: 29 also).

2. Verses which offer a different translation from that given in the main Greek text, while the translation in the main text stands in a position corresponding to that held by the corresponding material in the MT. Thus, v. 35[b] and 5: 10 (BM 4: 26) offer different translations of what is basically[5] the same Hebrew. In the MT the material appears at 5: 10.

3. Verses which offer a different translation from that given in the main Greek text, while the corresponding material in the MT agrees in position with neither translation. Thus v. 35[fβ] and 9: 9[a] and MT 9: 24 correspond in subject matter; but each stands in a completely different context.

3

4. Verses which offer a translation of material which is in the MT but entirely missing from the main Greek text. Thus v. 35^g presents a translation of material which in the MT stands at 9: 25, but which in the main Greek text is nowhere to be found.

5. Phrases, or verses, like v. 35^k, which have no counterpart either in the main Greek text or in the MT.

Now readings of this kind, if found scattered here and there in the margins or between the lines of a manuscript, would occasion no surprise; but to find them collected together and stationed in the middle of the on-going stream of narrative is an extraordinary thing. It is not as if they occurred thus in just one manuscript; they are found in practically all manuscripts, so that their entry into the text must have been fairly early. Nor does it appear that their presence in the text is the result of an accident: even a superficial glance will discover the following tell-tale evidence.

In the MT the execution of Shimei is related in two parts: Pt I in 2: 8–9, and Pt II in 2: 36–46. Now the main Greek text presents translations of these two parts, each stationed in a position that corresponds exactly to its MT counterpart. But vv. 35^{l-o} offer another and different translation of Pt I. In this they resemble many of the verses 35^{a-k} which, as we have just seen, offer different translations of other passages in the main Greek text; and it is reasonable to suppose that they may have had a similar origin. At the same time vv. 35^{l-o} are stationed immediately in front of vv. 36–46 which give the main text's translation of Pt II (and there is no second translation of Pt II given anywhere), so that vv. 35^{l-o} and 36–46 give the whole story of Shimei's execution in one uninterrupted flow. This is hardly accidental; but if vv. 35^{l-o} have been deliberately integrated with the main text in this way, it would be difficult to think that vv. 35^{a-k} held their present position by accident,[6] however seemingly odd it is.

But there is a further oddity. After the main Greek text has told Pt II of Shimei's execution, we find inserted in the text another collection of variants, numbered 46^{a-l}, similar in type and variety to the first lot. This is exceedingly odd. It is strange

4

enough to have a large collection of variants inserted in the text at all; but if it is going to be done, why have two collections standing in nearby, but separated, positions, and not simply one collection?

The very oddity of the phenomenon calls for a thorough investigation; and in addition there is hope that in the course of this investigation we may gain further insight into the history of the whole of the much disturbed text of 3 Reigns.

CHAPTER 2

THE THEMES OF THE MISCELLANIES

It will be convenient for the purpose of our investigation to adopt Montgomery's terminology and call vv. 35^{a-k} the first miscellany (hereafter Misc. 1) and vv. 46^{a-l} the second miscellany (hereafter Misc. 2). Our concern in this chapter will then be to demonstrate that whatever the sources of the material in the miscellanies may have been, the material as it now stands in the miscellanies has been arranged so that its details fit with as much relevance as possible into certain dominant themes.

Montgomery was the first to notice this. He concluded from his analysis of the miscellanies that 'these miscellanies grew up out of some rational summaries of the Solomonic history; the backbone of the first is a survey of Solomon's wisdom and his building operations; of the second a transcript of H [i.e. the Hebrew passage] 4: 20–5: 6'. In two recent articles, which I may be allowed very briefly to summarise here, I have tried to carry Montgomery's observations further.

In the first[1] I pointed out that each miscellany begins with a statement of Solomon's wisdom; each miscellany also uses in its first verse the sand of the sea shore as a simile, Misc. 1 to describe Solomon's wisdom, Misc. 2 to describe the number of Judah and Israel. Now in later midrashim the fact that one scripture likens Solomon's wisdom to the sand of the sea shore and another scripture likens the number of Israel to the sand of the sea shore is held to be significant: it is taken to imply that Solomon's wisdom equalled that of all Israel. I suggested therefore that a similar midrashic interest lay behind the placing of Solomon's wisdom, the sand of the sea shore and the number of Israel as the opening themes of the two miscellanies. I pointed out also that Pt I of the story of Shimei's execution is the part that stresses Solomon's wisdom in the whole episode, and I suggested that this common theme of Solomon's wisdom accounts for the duplication of Pt I of the Shimei story, and for the grouping of the miscellanies round that story.

In the second article[2] I endeavoured to show that whereas both miscellanies are concerned with Solomon's wisdom, Misc. 1 deals with his wisdom in his building activities, while Misc. 2 deals with his wisdom in government, administration and supplies, and I called attention to extensive evidence which suggests that the two miscellanies have not been left to stand as isolated islands, but have been integrated with the whole of the main text, and that their very existence and their incorporation into the main text are connected with the re-orderings and re-interpretations of the text that are such a pronounced feature of the whole of 3 Reigns.

But much more can be said to demonstrate that the two miscellanies are carefully constructed in order to develop certain themes. Here again is Misc. 1.

35ᵃ   ³⁵ᵃΚαὶ ἔδωκεν κύριος φρόνησιν τῷ Σαλωμων καὶ σοφίαν πολλὴν σφόδρα καὶ πλάτος καρδίας ὡς ἡ ἄμμος ἡ παρὰ τὴν θάλασσαν,
35ᵇ   ³⁵ᵇκαὶ ἐπληθύνθη ἡ φρόνησις Σαλωμων σφόδρα ὑπὲρ τὴν φρόνησιν
35ᶜ   πάντων ἀρχαίων υἱῶν καὶ ὑπὲρ πάντας φρονίμους Αἰγύπτου. ³⁵ᶜκαὶ ἔλαβεν τὴν θυγατέρα Φαραω καὶ εἰσήγαγεν αὐτὴν εἰς τὴν πόλιν Δαυιδ ἕως συντελέσαι αὐτὸν τὸν οἶκον αὐτοῦ καὶ τὸν οἶκον κυρίου ἐν πρώτοις καὶ τὸ τεῖχος Ιερουσαλημ κυκλόθεν· ἐν ἑπτὰ ἔτεσιν
35ᵈ   ἐποίησεν καὶ συνετέλεσεν. ³⁵ᵈκαὶ ἦν τῷ Σαλωμων ἑβδομήκοντα χιλιάδες αἴροντες ἄρσιν καὶ ὀγδοήκοντα χιλιάδες λατόμων ἐν τῷ
35ᵉ   ὄρει. ³⁵ᵉκαὶ ἐποίησεν Σαλωμων τὴν θάλασσαν καὶ τὰ ὑποστηρίγματα καὶ τοὺς λουτῆρας τοὺς μεγάλους καὶ τοὺς στύλους καὶ τὴν
35ᶠ   κρήνην τῆς αὐλῆς καὶ τὴν θάλασσαν τὴν χαλκῆν. ³⁵ᶠκαὶ ᾠκοδόμησεν τὴν ἄκραν καὶ τὰς ἐπάλξεις αὐτῆς καὶ διέκοψεν τὴν πόλιν Δαυιδ· οὕτως θυγάτηρ Φαραω ἀνέβαινεν ἐκ τῆς πόλεως Δαυιδ εἰς τὸν οἶκον αὐτῆς, ὃν ᾠκοδόμησεν αὐτῇ· τότε ᾠκοδόμησεν τὴν
35ᵍ   ἄκραν. ³⁵ᵍκαὶ Σαλωμων ἀνέφερεν τρεῖς ἐν τῷ ἐνιαυτῷ ὁλοκαυτώσεις καὶ εἰρηνικὰς ἐπὶ τὸ θυσιαστήριον, ὃ ᾠκοδόμησεν τῷ κυρίῳ, καὶ
35ʰ   ἐθυμία ἐνώπιον κυρίου. καὶ συνετέλεσεν τὸν οἶκον. ³⁵ʰκαὶ οὗτοι οἱ ἄρχοντες οἱ καθεσταμένοι ἐπὶ τὰ ἔργα τοῦ Σαλωμων· τρεῖς χιλιάδες καὶ ἑξακόσιοι ἐπιστάται τοῦ λαοῦ τῶν ποιούντων τὰ

35^i ἔργα. ^{35i}καὶ ᾠκοδόμησεν τὴν Ασσουρ καὶ τὴν Μαγδω καὶ τὴν
35^k Γαζερ καὶ τὴν Βαιθωρων τὴν ἐπάνω καὶ τὰ Βααλαθ· ^{35k}πλὴν μετὰ
τὸ οἰκοδομῆσαι αὐτὸν τὸν οἶκον τοῦ κυρίου καὶ τὸ τεῖχος Ιερουσαλημ κύκλῳ, μετὰ ταῦτα ᾠκοδόμησεν τὰς πόλεις ταύτας.

It is at once apparent that one idea – the finishing of the house
of the Lord and the timing of that finishing in relation to certain
other activities – repeats itself throughout the miscellany, in
vv. c, g and k. This could, of course, be nothing more than an
accidental coincidence, but there are several indications that it
is not.

1. If we compare v. c with its counterparts in the main
Greek text and in the MT we find as follows: the first part of
the verse (down to κυκλόθεν) has its counterpart in the MT at
3: 1, and in the main Greek text at 5: 14a (Rahlfs; 4: 31 BM);
the remainder of the verse has its counterpart in the MT at
6: 38^b, or so it would seem,[3] and no counterpart at all in the
main Greek text. This means that v. c is composite, that is, it is
made up of material which, as far as we can tell, originally
stood part in one context and part in another. That the two
parts now stand together in v. c is, therefore, presumably the
deliberate work of the editor of the miscellany. And this in turn
shows that the editor was particularly interested in how long it
took to build the house of the Lord and when it was finished.

2. The words ἐν πρώτοις in v. c^α are clearly concerned to tell
us that, in spite of the order of the phrase τὸν οἶκον αὐτοῦ καὶ
τὸν οἶκον Κυρίου, Solomon did in fact build the Lord's house
first before he built his own house. But the words have no
counterpart in either the MT or the main Greek text (in spite
of the fact that the rest of v. c^α has a counterpart in the main
Greek text). Their presence in the verse seems entirely due to
the editor and emphasises his interest in the length of time it
took to build the Lord's house and in when it was finished. It
also incidentally shows him in the rôle of a commentator, concerned to correct the impression which a reader might un-
wittingly receive from the order of the phrase in the MT – his
own house and the Lord's house – that Solomon built his own
house first.[4]

3. V. k likewise has no counterpart in either the MT or the main Greek text. It is plainly editorial comment, and is concerned to establish that certain cities which Solomon built were not built before the Lord's house. Clearly the theme continues by the editor's deliberate intention. But, then, why should anybody ever think that these cities were built before the Lord's house? Why the need for the explicit and emphatic statement? The answer appears to be this: in the paragraph in the MT in which the building of these cities is recorded, the building of these cities is mentioned *before* the record of the completion of the Lord's house; and therefore the editor of the miscellany, in taking over a good deal of material from this paragraph, is at pains to forestall, or correct, any wrong impression that might be obtained from the order of the MT. It is the fact that not only v. i but vv. f$^{\beta\gamma}$, g and h all find their counterpart in the MT in the paragraph 9: 15–25 thus:

MT ch. 9		Misc. 1
vv. 15, 17	Building of cities	v. i
v. 23	Solomon's chief officers	v. h
v. 24	Pharaoh's daughter	v. f$^{\beta\gamma}$
v. 25	Solomon's thrice-yearly offerings: 'and he finished the house'	v. g

It will be at once noticed that in the MT the paragaph *begins* with the building of the cities and *ends* with the mention of the completion of the Lord's house. Not so, of course, the miscellany. The building of the cities is there stationed *after* the mention of the completion of the Lord's house. And the editor has not even so been content to make his point by simply making this change of order; he has added in v. k an editorial comment that states his point explicitly. So once more we notice that the editor was not just some tidy-minded scribe, who, finding a number of stray variants, grouped them in some rough and ready logical order. He was a commentator, commenting here on the order of the text that we find in the MT.

4. Returning to v. c we find another revealing clue showing that the miscellany has been put together by an editor accord-

ing to a carefully thought out scheme. Verse c is concerned to tell us that Solomon brought Pharaoh's daughter into the city of David until he finished building his own house, the house of the Lord and the wall of Jerusalem. Now a later verse in the miscellany tells us that eventually Pharaoh's daughter came up out of the city of David into her house which Solomon built for her (verse f). It could, of course, be a sheer accident that two of the variant translations with which the editor had to cope happened to be about Pharaoh's daughter and her arrival in, and departure from, her temporary residence in the city of David. But granted this much is an accident, it seems fairly certain that the *positioning* of these two items in the miscellany is no accident. Consider the sweep of the 'narrative':

35ᶜ   ³⁵ᶜΚαὶ ἔλαβεν τὴν θυγατέρα Φαραω καὶ εἰσήγαγεν αὐτὴν εἰς τὴν πόλιν Δαυιδ ἕως συντελέσαι αὐτὸν τὸν οἶκον αὐτοῦ καὶ τὸν οἶκον κυρίου ἐν πρώτοις καὶ τὸ τεῖχος Ιερουσαλημ κυκλόθεν· ἐν ἑπτὰ

35ᵈ   ἔτεσιν ἐποίησεν καὶ συνετέλεσεν. ³⁵ᵈκαὶ ἦν τῷ Σαλωμων ἑβδομή-κοντα χιλιάδες αἴροντες ἄρσιν καὶ ὀγδοήκοντα χιλιάδες λατόμων

35ᵉ   ἐν τῷ ὄρει. ³⁵ᵉΚαὶ ἐποίησεν Σαλωμων τὴν θάλασσαν καὶ τὰ ὑποστηρίγματα καὶ τοὺς λουτῆρας τοὺς μεγάλους καὶ τοὺς στύ-λους καὶ τὴν κρήνην τῆς αὐλῆς καὶ τὴν θάλασσαν τὴν χαλκῆν.

35ᶠ   ³⁵ᶠΚαὶ ᾠκοδόμησεν τὴν ἄκραν καὶ τὰς ἐπάλξεις αὐτῆς καὶ διέκοψεν τὴν πόλιν Δαυιδ· οὕτως θυγάτηρ Φαραω ἀνέβαινεν ἐκ τῆς πόλεως Δαυιδ εἰς τὸν οἶκον αὐτῆς, ὃν ᾠκοδόμησεν αὐτῇ· τότε ᾠκοδόμησεν τὴν ἄκραν.

Clearly, as it stands, v. fᵝ is intended to complete the story begun in v. c; for, after v. c has remarked that Pharaoh's daughter's stay in David's city was meant to last only until certain buildings were built, the verses intervening between v. c and v. fᵝ are all without exception concerned with the erection of these buildings: v. cᵝ with the time it took to build, namely seven years; v. d with the labour force required for the job; v. e with sundry items of furniture in the house of the Lord that had to be built first; v. f with Millo, its fortifications (part of the fortification complex of Jerusalem; cf. LXX 10: 23 ...τὸ τεῖχος Ιερουσαλημ καὶ τὴν ἄκραν) and the city of David.

Moreover, that the arranging of these intervening verses in their present position is due to the editor and his deliberate scheme, is shown by a further consideration. If one looks at the miscellany as a whole, one will see that some verses stand together in the miscellany just as they do in the main text. Verses a and b, for instance, are the counterparts of verses 9 and 10 of ch. 5 (MT and LXX Rahlfs; BM verses 25 and 26 of ch. 4) and they stand together in the miscellany just as verses 9 and 10 of ch. 5 do in the main text. Doubtless they entered the miscellany together as one block of material. But the verses intervening between v. c^α and v. f^β are a collection of items that, as far as we can see, never stood together anywhere before they were put together here in the miscellany: v. c^β seems to be[5] the counterpart of MT 6: 38[b] and has no counterpart in the main LXX text; v. d is the counterpart of MT 5: 29 and the word for word doublet of the main Greek text at 5: 29 (Rahlfs; BM 5: 15); v. e is a medley of small details taken from various places in ch. 7; and v. f^α is an alternative translation of 11: 27 (MT and LXX). One can only conclude that this medley of material now stands together where it does, because the editor of the miscellany saw that it all concerned the building that had to be done between the time of Pharaoh's daughter's entry into the city of David and her departure therefrom.

And there is yet a further piece of evidence. Consider again the block of material vv. f^β, g and h. Why does its internal order differ from that of its counterpart in the MT? The MT's order is:

1. 9: 23   Solomon's chief officers.
2.   24   Pharaoh's daughter's departure from David's city.
3.   25   Solomon's thrice-yearly offerings.

The miscellany has:

1. v. f^β Pharaoh's daughter's departure.
2. v. g   Solomon's thrice-yearly offerings.
3. v. h   Solomon's chief officers.

It seems obvious that in the miscellany the item about Pharaoh's daughter has been re-arranged to stand first so that it could appropriately continue the daughter-of-Pharaoh theme begun in v. c.

Misc. 1, then, is a very carefully constructed piece of work. Its theme is in general Solomon's wisdom in his building activities, and in particular his wisdom in completing the Lord's house before he built his own house, his wife's house or any of the cities which he built. Moreover, we have seen that the construction of the miscellany was the work not merely of a scribe but of a Biblical commentator. That a commentator should be thus concerned to expound the theme of the completion of the temple is, of course, nothing surprising. The *Pesikta Rabbati*, of much later times, has eight discourses for the Feast of Dedication, and the sixth one of them is a commentary on the verse, 'Thus all the work that Solomon wrought in the house of the Lord was finished'; this commentary does not fail, of course, to point out (section 4) that Solomon finished the Lord's house before he started his own. But interest in the Biblical passages that speak of the completion and dedication of the Lord's house did not first arise in these later times; the establishment of the Feast of Hanukkah (1 Macc. 4: 59) must have led to an immediate and intense interest in them, since doubtless the reading of scriptures appropriate to the rededication must from the very first have formed part of the annual celebration.

We turn now to Misc. 2. Here it is again.

46ª   ⁴⁶ªΚαὶ ἦν ὁ βασιλεὺς Σαλωμων φρόνιμος σφόδρα καὶ σοφός, καὶ
Ιουδα καὶ Ισραηλ πολλοὶ σφόδρα ὡς ἡ ἄμμος ἡ ἐπὶ τῆς θαλάσ-
46ᵇ   σης εἰς πλῆθος, ἐσθίοντες καὶ πίνοντες καὶ χαίροντες· ⁴⁶ᵇκαὶ Σαλωμων ἦν ἄρχων ἐν πάσαις ταῖς βασιλείαις, καὶ ἦσαν προσφέροντες
δῶρα καὶ ἐδούλευον τῷ Σαλωμων πάσας τὰς ἡμέρας τῆς ζωῆς
46ᶜ   αὐτοῦ. ⁴⁶ᶜκαὶ Σαλωμων ἤρξατο διανοίγειν τὰ δυναστεύματα
46ᵈ   τοῦ Λιβάνου, ⁴⁶ᵈκαὶ αὐτὸς ᾠκοδόμησεν τὴν Θερμαι ἐν τῇ ἐρήμῳ.
46ᵉ   ⁴⁶ᵉκαὶ τοῦτο τὸ ἄριστον τῷ Σαλωμων· τριάκοντα κόροι σεμιδάλεως
καὶ ἑξήκοντα κόροι ἀλεύρου κεκοπανισμένου, δέκα μόσχοι ἐκλεκτοὶ
καὶ εἴκοσι βόες νομάδες καὶ ἑκατὸν πρόβατα ἐκτὸς ἐλάφων καὶ

46ᶠ δορκάδων καὶ ὀρνίθων ἐκλεκτῶν νομάδων. ⁴⁶ᶠὅτι ἦν ἄρχων ἐν
παντὶ πέραν τοῦ ποταμοῦ ἀπὸ Ραφι ἕως Γάζης, ἐν πᾶσιν τοῖς
46ᵍ βασιλεῦσιν πέραν τοῦ ποταμοῦ· ⁴⁶ᵍκαὶ ἦν αὐτῷ εἰρήνη ἐκ πάντων
τῶν μερῶν αὐτοῦ κυκλόθεν, καὶ κατῴκει Ιουδα καὶ Ισραηλ πεποιθότες, ἕκαστος ὑπὸ τὴν ἄμπελον αὐτοῦ καὶ ὑπὸ τὴν συκῆν αὐτοῦ,
ἐσθίοντες καὶ πίνοντες, ἀπὸ Δαν καὶ ἕως Βηρσαβεε πάσας τὰς
46ʰ ἡμέρας Σαλωμων. — ⁴⁶ʰκαὶ οὗτοι οἱ ἄρχοντες τοῦ Σαλωμων·
Αζαριου υἱὸς Σαδωκ τοῦ ἱερέως καὶ Ορνιου υἱὸς Ναθαν ἄρχων τῶν
ἐφεστηκότων καὶ Εδραμ ἐπὶ τὸν οἶκον αὐτοῦ καὶ Σουβα γραμματεὺς καὶ Βασα υἱὸς Αχιθαλαμ ἀναμιμνήσκων καὶ Αβι υἱὸς Ιωαβ
ἀρχιστράτηγος καὶ Αχιρε υἱὸς Εδραϊ ἐπὶ τὰς ἄρσεις καὶ Βαναια
υἱὸς Ιωδαε ἐπὶ τῆς αὐλαρχίας καὶ ἐπὶ τοῦ πλινθείου καὶ Ζαχουρ
46ⁱ υἱὸς Ναθαν ὁ σύμβουλος. — ⁴⁶ⁱκαὶ ἦσαν τῷ Σαλωμων τεσσαράκοντα
χιλιάδες τοκάδες ἵπποι εἰς ἅρματα καὶ δώδεκα χιλιάδες ἱππέων.
46ᵏ ⁴⁶ᵏκαὶ ἦν ἄρχων ἐν πᾶσιν τοῖς βασιλεῦσιν ἀπὸ τοῦ ποταμοῦ καὶ
ἕως γῆς ἀλλοφύλων καὶ ἕως ὁρίων Αἰγύπτου.
46ˡ ⁴⁶ˡΣαλωμων υἱὸς Δαυιδ ἐβασίλευσεν ἐπὶ Ισραηλ καὶ Ιουδα ἐν
Ιερουσαλημ.

It takes no more than a glance to see that there is a dominant
theme running through this miscellany: the wisdom of Solomon's government and the peace and prosperity that resulted
from his extensive dominions abroad. But since Montgomery is
quite correct in saying[6] that Misc. 2 is largely a transcript of
the Hebrew[7] passage 4: 20–5: 6, which deals likewise with the
same theme, it might be thought that the presence of this theme
in Misc. 2 is due not to the editor, but to his source. And so to a
large extent it is. On the other hand there are not wanting a
number of indications that the editor has gone out of his way
to develop and emphasise the theme presented to him by his
source material.

First take the wisdom theme with which the miscellany
opens. As we have already seen,[8] it balances very neatly the
opening wisdom theme of Misc. 1. But observe how this
balance has been contrived. After its initial comment on
Solomon's wisdom, Misc. 2 includes material that finds its
counterpart in the first six verses of MT 5: 1–6 (EVV 4: 20–6)
thus:

$$\text{Misc. 2 v. b} = \text{MT 5: } 1^{a \text{ and } c}$$
$$\text{v. e} = \quad 2\text{--}3$$
$$\text{v. f} = \quad 4^a$$
$$\text{v. g} = \quad 4^b, 5$$
$$\text{v. i} = \quad 6$$

Now it so happens that MT 5: 9–10 is a wisdom passage: 'And God gave wisdom to Solomon and understanding exceeding much, and breadth of heart like the sand which is on the sea shore.' If, then, Misc. 2 was interested in Solomon's wisdom, and if it incorporated the MT's material from verses 1 to 6 of ch. 5, why did it not proceed to incorporate vv. 9–10 as well, seeing they too speak of Solomon's wisdom? The reason is obvious: the counterpart of MT 5: 9–10 is the verses which stand at the beginning of Misc. 1 (v. 35ᵃ = 5: 9, v. 35ᵇ = 5: 10). If vv. 9–10 had been placed in Misc. 2 there would have been no balance between the miscellanies at all: Misc. 1 would have lacked reference to Solomon's wisdom, and Misc. 2 would have contained the sand-of-the-sea-shore simile twice over. Quite clearly, editorial planning has avoided this potential clumsiness, and achieved in the process not only a neat balance, but, as we earlier saw, a midrashic point.

Secondly the opening phrase of Misc. 2, which secures that the miscellany shall begin with a notice of Solomon's wisdom, and, incidentally, draws such a deliberate parallel – Σαλωμων φρόνιμος σφόδρα...καὶ Ιουδα καὶ Ισραηλ πολλοὶ σφόδρα – is from one point of view suspect. Its words – καὶ ἦν ὁ βασιλεὺς Σαλωμων φρόνιμος σφόδρα καὶ σοφός – have no exact counterpart either in the MT or in the main Greek text. Certainly the theme of the clause is found elsewhere, but the exact words not. Of course, the clause may be founded on a non-MT Hebrew; but since Misc. 1 has shown instances of pure editorial comment, a suspicion is raised that v. aᵅ of Misc. 2 is an editorial adaptation in the interests of the editor's scheme.

Thirdly, we find a similar phenomenon in the last verse of the miscellany, Σαλωμων υἱὸς Δαυιδ ἐβασίλευσεν ἐπὶ Ισραηλ καὶ Ιουδα ἐν Ιερουσαλημ: it has no exact counterpart either in the

MT or in the main Greek text. There is something superficially similar in MT 4: 1: 'And king Solomon was king over all Israel', and of this the main Greek text at 4: 1 has an almost identical counterpart, καὶ ἦν ὁ βασιλεὺς Σαλωμων βασιλεύων ἐπὶ Ισραηλ (though it distorts the picture by putting 'Israel', instead of 'all Israel', a fault which 2: 46¹ avoids by putting ἐπὶ Ισραηλ καὶ Ιουδα, the equivalent of *all* Israel). But over the more significant details – ἐβασίλευσεν...ἐν Ιερουσαλημ, and Σαλωμων υἱὸς Δαυιδ – v. 46¹ is different from both the MT and the main Greek text. Normally the phrase, X *son of* Y occurs only in the accession formula[9] of any particular king. Elsewhere during the history of his reign it is enough to refer to the king simply as X. Now the use in v. 46¹ of the phrase Σαλωμων υἱὸς Δαυιδ ἐβασίλευσεν may in fact mean that the verse is based on a non-MT type Hebrew text which used the accession formula for Solomon whereas the MT does not. But even so it is still inept to station an *accession* formula at the end of a miscellany which has already spoken several times of the wide extent of Solomon's dominion, and itself follows the story of the execution of Shimei which took place *after* Solomon's accession. Similarly, there are usually in the accession formulae of the kings of Judah two (among other) elements.

1. The phrase: 'X son of Y began to reign over Judah'. Here the verb is, in the γγ section of Reigns, normally, but not always,[10] translated by the present tense, βασιλεύει.

2. The phrase: 'and Z years did X reign in Jerusalem'. Here the verb is uniformly in the aorist. The sentence in v. 46¹, therefore – Σαλωμων υἱὸς Δαυιδ ἐβασίλευσεν ἐπὶ Ισραηλ καὶ Ιουδα ἐν Ιερουσαλημ – seems to be a conflate of these two elements in the normal accession formula.

Standing then at the *end* of the miscellany, it is, we may repeat, very oddly placed. But if we forget for a moment that it was originally an accession formula, it is easy to see that *in the miscellany* the verse holds a very deliberate and reasonable position. The dominant theme of the miscellany, as we have seen, is the extent of Solomon's reign. The other references in the miscellany to Solomon's reign, vv. 46[b, f and k], all explicitly deal with his rule *abroad*; v. 1, on the other hand, explicitly talks of his rule *at home* 'over Israel and Judah in Jerusalem'. And seeing that the main narrative which immediately follows v. 1 is going to talk for the most part of Solomon's rule at home, v. 1 provides a fitting introduction – fitting, that is, if one forgets that it seems originally to be based on the accession formula and therefore should have come immediately at the beginning of the narrative of Solomon's reign.

Fourthly, consider vv. c and d: (v. c) καὶ Σαλωμων ἤρξατο διανοίγειν τὰ δυναστεύματα τοῦ Λιβάνου, (v. d) καὶ αὐτὸς ᾠκοδόμησεν τὴν Θερμαι ἐν τῇ ἐρήμῳ. These verses, in so far as they have a counterpart in the MT, come from an entirely different context from that of the rest of the material in Misc. 2. Presumably, then, the fact that they stand in Misc. 2 and not in Misc. 1 may be directly attributed to the editor. And this presumption is strengthened when we observe that v. d certainly, and v. c probably, come originally from the same context as v. i of Misc. 1. That context is, in the MT, 9: 15–19, and, in the main Greek text, 10: 22ª (Rahlfs; BM 10: 23, 24). It lists a number of cities built by Solomon: Hazor, Megiddo, Gezer, Beth-horon the nether, Baalath, Tamar 'in the wilderness, in the land'. Of these cities v. i of Misc. 1 has Hazor (Ασσουρ), Megiddo (Μαγδω), Gezer (Γαзερ), Beth-horon (which, however, it calls 'the upper' instead of 'the nether', Βαιθωρων τὴν ἐπάνω) and Baalath (τὰ Βααλαθ); but it has no mention of Tamar. Misc. 2, on the other hand, has none of the other cities, but it has Tamar in the wilderness (τὴν Θερμαι ἐν τῇ ἐρήμῳ). Now the identity of this city, Tamar, presents an interesting problem. Montgomery argued[11] that it was at the southern boundary of the Holy Land and that the MT's seemingly strange description 'in the wilderness in the land' made sense if understood as meaning 'Tamar-in-the-Steppe in the Land'. On this understanding Tamar was *inside* the nation's boundaries. But, as Montgomery pointed out, the Ķrê in 1 Kings 10 and the Kethîb of 2 Chron. 8: 4 spell the name 'Tadmor'; and the Greek of Misc. 2, Θερμαι, and of the main text, 10: 23, Ιεθερμαθ (אֶת־ח'), both are based on a Hebrew

תדמר read as תרמר. In fact, in both places Lucianic manuscripts have Θοδμορ. This points to an early identification of the town with Tadmor-Palmyra, which famous city lay, of course, *outside* the nation's boundaries. It was, as Josephus in his comment on I Kings 10 describes it, 'in the desert above Syria'. Now it is noticeable that v. d of Misc. 2 has simply τὴν Θερμαι ἐν τῇ ἐρήμῳ; it does not add 'in the land' as the MT does. To the editor this city was, it seems, not in the land, but outside it. Moreover v. c, which the editor places immediately in front of this record of building Θερμαι, is explicitly concerned with Solomon's activities in the Lebanon.[12] This 'pairing together "the fortresses of the Lebanon and Thodmor (so the Lucianic MSS) in the desert"', as Montgomery puts it, strengthens the impression that for the editor Θερμαι (or Θοδμορ) was in foreign parts.

With this we come to the point of this long discussion. The fact is that the cities have been divided up so that the fortresses of the Lebanon and Θερμαι-in-the-desert stand together in Misc. 2, while all the other cities are stationed in Misc. 1. The explanation of the fact seems obvious: Misc. 2, witness vv. b, f and k, is very much concerned with Solomon's *foreign* do-minions. The fortresses of the Lebanon and Θερμαι-in-the-wilderness, being regarded as situated in foreign parts, are therefore placed in Misc. 2, and that directly after v. b, which mentions the foreign dominions and the income which accrued to Solomon from them. The other cities, being situated in the homeland, are stationed in Misc. 1, which deals with Solomon's domestic building programme.

Such detailed care in the organisation of his basic material shows that the editor was in Misc. 2, just as in Misc. 1, working with a definite theme in his mind. Further evidence to this effect could be cited, but since that evidence is even more germane to the topic of our next chapter, it will be discussed there.

CHAPTER 3

INSTANCES OF MIDRASHIC
EXEGESIS IN THE MISCELLANIES

A preliminary observation: the methods of midrashic exegesis
are not such as readily commend themselves to the modern
western mind. To say no more, midrash is inclined to see implications, allusions and significant connections of thought where
the modern mind cannot – indeed where the modern mind
would stoutly deny that any existed. The modern scholar, then,
would rightly regard midrashic methods as illegitimate in his
own efforts to elucidate the meaning of Scripture. But if we are
to track down the work of an ancient midrashically-minded
editor, we must be prepared to think midrashically as he did.
Admittedly there is then the danger that we shall outdo the
ancients and read into the text midrashic significance which we
have ourselves invented and which no ancient ever dreamed
of – but then there are not lacking nowadays an abundance of
modern minds, untainted with midrash, who can happily
correct this dangerous error, should it occur.

As my first instance of midrashic exegesis I take Misc. 1 v. f,
which I quote from the text of Vaticanus B and not from
Rahlfs' edition (from which I have hitherto quoted).[1] καὶ
ᾠκοδόμησεν τὴν ἄκραν ἔπαλξιν ἐπ' αὐτῆς· διέκοψεν τὴν πόλιν
Δαυειδ. οὕτως θυγάτηρ Φαραω ἀνέβαινεν ἐκ τῆς πόλεως Δαυειδ
εἰς τὸν οἶκον αὐτῆς ὃν ᾠκοδόμησεν αὐτῇ. τότε ᾠκοδόμησεν τὴν
ἄκραν.

The first thing to notice is that v. f is made up of two elements
drawn from different contexts. Element (a), as will be demonstrated in a moment, finds its counterpart in the Jeroboam
story, at 11:27 in the MT, and in the main Greek text similarly
at 11:27. It extends as far as διέκοψεν τὴν πόλιν Δαυειδ.
Element (b), from οὕτως to the end of the verse, finds its
counterpart in the MT in a completely different context at

9: 24; in the main Greek text there is no exact equivalent.[2] The reason why the editor of the miscellany has put the two elements together is obviously because Element (a) begins καὶ ᾠκοδόμησεν τὴν ἄκραν, and Element (b) ends τότε ᾠκοδόμησεν τὴν ἄκραν.

The next thing to notice is that Element (a) is an absurd mistranslation of its Hebrew, which is the more remarkable since the Hebrew is straightforward and correctly translated by the main Greek text:

v. f	MT	Gk 11: 27
καὶ	שְׁלֹמֹה	Σαλωμων
ᾠκοδόμησεν	בָּנָה	ᾠκοδόμησεν
τὴν ἄκραν	אֶת־הַמִּלּוֹא	τὴν ἄκραν·
ἔπαλξιν (ἐπ᾿ αὐτῆς)	סָגַר	συνέκλεισεν
	אֶת־	τὸν
διέκοψεν	פֶּרֶץ	φραγμὸν
τὴν πόλιν Δαυειδ.	עִיר־דָּוִד	τῆς πόλεως Δαυειδ
	אָבִיו	τοῦ πατρὸς αὐτοῦ.

The mystery of how the translator of v. f came by this bizarre translation has long since been explained by Klostermann and Montgomery:[3] סגר את has been read as one word and given the meaning of מִסְגֶּרֶת, 'fortress', 'rampart'; פרץ has been read as פָּרַץ; ἐπ᾿ αὐτῆς has been added to help out the sense.[4] A question which we will have to face in a moment, however, is whether this bizarre translation was simply a mistake or whether it was arrived at by a deliberate manipulation of the Hebrew.

Meanwhile we must look at οὕτως, the word which, as they now stand, seems quite obviously intended to connect Element (b) to Element (a): ' ...he cut through (made a break in) the city of David; *in this way* the daughter of Pharaoh came up out of the city of David'. As far as we can tell, οὕτως has no Hebrew authority. The counterpart in the MT to Element (b) is to be found at 9: 24. A similar Hebrew occurs in 2 Chron. 8: 11. These two Hebrew passages and the varying Greek translations of them are set out on the next page.

19

MT 1 Kings 9: 24	LXX 3 Reigns 2: 35ᶠ	LXX 3 Reigns 9: 9a	MT 2 Chron. 8: 11	LXX 2 Paralip. 8: 11
אַךְ	οὕτως	τότε	וְאֶת־	καὶ τὴν
בַּת־	θυγάτηρ	ἀνήγαγεν	בַּת־פַּר"	θυγατέρα Φ.
פַּרְעֹה	Φαραω	Σαλωμων	הֶעֱלָה	Σαλωμων
עָלְתָה	ἀνέβαινεν	τὴν θυγατέρα Φ.	שְׁלֹמֹה	ἀνήγαγεν
מֵעִיר	ἐκ τῆς πόλεως	ἐκ πόλεως	מֵעִיר	ἐκ πόλεως
דָּוִד	Δαυιδ	Δαυιδ	דָּוִיד	Δαυιδ
אֶל־	εἰς τὸν	εἰς		εἰς τὸν
בֵּיתָהּ	οἶκον αὐτῆς	οἶκον αὐτοῦ	לַבַּיִת	οἶκον
אֲשֶׁר	ὃν	ὃν	אֲשֶׁר	ὃν
בָּנָה־	ᾠκοδόμησεν	ᾠκοδόμησεν	בָּנָה־	ᾠκοδόμησεν
לָהּ	αὐτῇ.	αὐτῷ	לָהּ	αὐτῇ
אָז	τότε	ἐν		
בָּנָה	ᾠκοδόμησεν	ταῖς		
אֶת־	τὴν	ἡμέραις		
הַמִּלּוֹא:	ἄκραν	ἐκείναις.		

It will be seen that whereas v. f naturally disagrees with the Hebrew of Chronicles (though 9: 9a is much nearer to it),[5] it agrees in every detail of meaning and word-order with the Hebrew of 1 Kings 9: 24 except for its first word: οὕτως does not represent אַךְ. If based on a Hebrew text at all, οὕτως would go back to a כֹּה or a כֵּן, more probably to the latter. But then it is very difficult to think of a context anywhere in the Hebrew of 1 Kings where the coming up of Pharaoh's daughter could be introduced by כֵּן *in this way, so*. One is therefore led to the conclusion that οὕτως is the work of the editor of the miscellany, who put Element (a) and Element (b) together not merely because they both mentioned the same things, but because he intended Element (b) *to explain* Element (a): 'he made a breach in the city of David; *in this way* Pharaoh's daughter came up out of the city of David'.

It might well be objected, of course, that this 'explanation' is neither fair to Scripture nor true to history, and that it is in itself absurd. Quite so, according to our standards; but it is perfectly in keeping with the methods and spirit of midrash. Consider by way of comparison, another comment[6] on the very verse, 11: 27, of which our v. f is a variant translation. 'Jeroboam...reproved Solomon...As it is written,...*Solomon built Millo, and repaired the breaches of the city of David his father.* He said thus to him: Thy father David made breaches in the wall, that Israel might come up [to Jerusalem] on the Festivals; whilst thou hast closed them, in order to exact toll for the benefit of Pharaoh's daughter.' In detail this is different from our v. f, which has it that it was Solomon who made a breach in the city, and that he did so in order to get Pharaoh's daughter out of it. But the spirit of the two comments is the same; and both are equally absurd.

Now since we can with a fair amount of certainty trace to the editor this much of midrashic interpretation, there may be no harm in speculating about what further midrashic principles may have guided him in the compilation of the verse.

First, he may have been moved by the idea that there is significance in the juxtaposition of two events in Scripture. Not all ancient rabbis derived lessons from juxtaposition,[7] but the method was very frequently used nevertheless. Take one example from Numbers:

20: 14–21. From Kadesh Israel sends a request to the king of Edom to be allowed to pass through his land. The request is refused.

22. Israel leaves Kadesh and comes to Mount Hor.

23–9. Aaron dies.

The fact that Aaron died at this juncture would to our minds not necessarily be connected with the Edom episode by anything more than chronological sequence. But hear the comment in the Midrash Rabbah:[8] 'Because Israel had associated themselves with the wicked nation in order to pass through their land, they lost a righteous man [i.e. Aaron]. For this reason the section dealing with Aaron's being gathered to his people immediately follows the section dealing with the king of Edom.'

Perhaps, then, the editor applied this technique to our v. f. Element (b) contains two parts:

1. In this way Pharaoh's daughter came up out of the city of David into her house which he (had) built for her.

2. Then he built the Akra.

Now why does the second part say that the building of the Akra took place when Pharaoh's daughter came up out of the city of David? Clearly the historical record need only imply that the one thing happened round about the same time as the other with no further connection between them. But a 'juxtaposition-exegete' would not have been satisfied with this; there must have been some deeper reason.[9]

To ferret out this reason our editor may then have applied the very common midrashic method that tries to solve a difficulty in one text by comparing that text with another text which has points of general similarity.[10] Verse f mentioned the city of David and the Akra; so he looked around for another verse that should mention the city of David and the Akra, and found it in 11: 27. But that verse in the Hebrew simply said 'Solomon built the Millo, he closed up (סָגַר) the breach of (אֶת־פֶּרֶץ) the city of David'. As it stood, therefore, 'closing up the breach' of the city of David did not seem to have any connection with Pharaoh's daughter's exit from that city. So the editor made use of yet other devices for interpretation, repointing and re-division of words and the replacing of one word by another similarly sounding word,[11] and so produced 'And he built the Akra, a battlement (מִסְגֶּרֶת) over it; (for) he (had) made a breach in (פָּרַץ) the city of David (and) in this way the daughter of Pharaoh came up out of the city of David into her house which he (had) built for her; then [i.e. when the breach had been made and she had gone out through it] he built the Akra.' It might even be (since, on this showing the editor was working with a Hebrew text before him) that he was also thinking of the literal meaning of אֶת־הַמִּלּוֹא (the Hebrew behind τὴν ἄκραν) namely 'something which fills up, a terrasse', and so meant to suggest that the Millo was built to plug the gap made in the city wall for Pharaoh's daughter's exit.[12]

Our speculation cannot, of course, give us certainty; it may not even be correct. But what does seem certain is that the uniting of the two elements in v. f by an editorial οὕτως is part of a deliberate attempt to explain one element by the other.

For a second instance of midrashic exegesis I refer once more to Misc. 2 and its dominant theme. Here are the verses that record the extent of Solomon's dominion:

v. 46ᵇ

καὶ Σαλωμων ἦν ἄρχων ἐν πάσαις ταῖς βασιλείαις καὶ ἦσαν προσφέροντες δῶρα καὶ ἐδούλευον τῷ Σαλωμων πάσας τὰς ἡμέρας τῆς ζωῆς αὐτοῦ.

v. 46ᶠ

ὅτι ἦν ἄρχων ἐν παντὶ πέραν τοῦ ποταμοῦ ἀπὸ Ραφι ἕως Γάζης ἐν πᾶσιν τοῖς βασιλεῦσιν πέραν τοῦ ποταμοῦ.

v. 46ᵏ

καὶ ἦν ἄρχων ἐν πάσιν τοῖς βασιλεῦσιν ἀπὸ τοῦ ποταμοῦ καὶ ἕως γῆς ἀλλοφύλων καὶ ἕως ὁρίων Αἰγύπτου.

v. 46ˡ

Σαλωμων υἱὸς Δαυιδ ἐβασίλευσεν ἐπὶ Ισραηλ καὶ Ιουδα ἐν Ιερουσαλημ.

Before we study these verses, we should remind ourselves that one of the multitudinous topics discussed by later rabbis was the increase and subsequent decrease of the extent of Solomon's dominion. The Midrash Rabbah,[13] *Song of Solomon*, I. I. 10, for instance, observes that Solomon rose by three stages. 'Of the first stage it is written, *For he had dominion over all the region on this side the River* (1 Kings v. 4). Of the second stage it says, *And Solomon ruled* (ib. 1). Of the third stage it says, *Then Solomon sat on the throne of the Lord as king* (1 Chron. XXIX. 23).' Of the decreasing stages of his rule, it says:

Solomon suffered three declines. The first decline was that after he had been a great king ruling from one end of the world to the other, his power was curtailed and he ruled only over Israel, for so it is written, *The Proverbs of Solomon son of David, king of Israel* (Prov. I. 1). The second decline was that after he had been king of Israel his power was reduced and he was left king only over Jerusalem, as it is written, *I Koheleth have been king over Israel in Jerusalem* (Eccl. I. 12). The third decline was that after he had been king over Jerusalem his power was reduced and he was left king only over his own household, as it says, *Behold it is the litter of Solomon, threescore mighty men are about it of the mighty men of Israel, they all handle the sword* (S.S. III. 7, 8); even over his own couch he was not king, for he feared the spirits.

Elsewhere the decreasing stages are worked out somewhat differently. The Babylonian Talmud, *Sanhedrin*, 20b, for example, has a scheme of five descending stages thus:

1. Reigned over the higher beings: he *sat on the throne of the Lord* (1 Chron. 28: 23).

2. Reigned only over the lower beings: *For he had dominion over all the region on this side the River, from Tifsah even to Gaza* (1 Kings 5: 4 MT).

3. Reign restricted to Israel: *I, Koheleth, have been king over Israel in Jerusalem* (Eccl. 1: 12).

4. Reign only over his couch: *Behold it is the litter of Solomon...* (S.S. 3: 7).

5. Reign only over his staff: *This was my portion from all my labour* (Eccl. 2: 10).

Moreover, this same passage in the Babylonian Talmud records a difference of opinion among the sages as to whether Solomon was first king, then commoner, then king again, or whether he was simply first king, then commoner. But differences of this sort in the Midrashim and the Talmud merely indicate how popular the topic was and how much it must have been debated.

Now when we look at the four verses in Misc. 2 relating to the extent of Solomon's dominion, we find that if they are approached in the same midrashic spirit, they too readily form a progression, marking the steadily decreasing extent of Solomon's dominion.

1. V. b: over all the kingdoms, without specified limit; that is, therefore, over the whole world.

2. V. f: over all the kings within certain limits.

3. V. k: over all the kings within certain differently described limits, certainly not greater, probably less, than the limits described in 2.

4. V. l: simply over Israel and Judah in Jerusalem.

We cannot, of course, decide without further question that the editor of Misc. 2 did view these verses in this way. Quite apart from the fact that he was working long before the formation of the Midrash Rabbah and the Babylonian Talmud, there is the crucial consideration that in order to form the verses into a progression, one must be prepared in the manner of the Talmud and Midrash to read into the verses a meaning which was never originally intended; and we cannot just assume that our editor did read such a meaning into them. The plain straightforward meaning of v. l, for example, can be seen by comparing it with the many other such verses to be found in 1 and 2 Kings. When, for instance, 2 Kings 15: 32 says: 'In the second year of Pekah...king of Israel began Jotham the son of Uzziah...to reign...and he reigned sixteen years in Jerusalem', the phrase 'in Jerusalem' is not intended to define the *extent* of his dominion, or to contrast his reign 'in Jerusalem' with his reign elsewhere. Similarly when 2 Kings 15: 17 says: 'In the thirty-ninth year of Azariah...began Menahem the son of Gadi to reign over Israel', the phrase 'over Israel' is not meant to imply that of course he once ruled over a much larger territory, but now he was reduced to ruling simply over Israel. Nor was Eccl. 1: 12, 'I, Koheleth, have been king over Israel in Jerusalem', originally intended to mean 'in Jerusalem, but not outside it'. True, the Midrash Rabbah chooses to make 'in Jerusalem' the operative phrase in the verse, and then arbitrarily and unreasonably treats it as limiting the scope of the previous phrase 'over Israel'; but this is not the original, nor even an obvious, meaning of the verse. Similarly with v. l of Misc. 2: 'Solomon, son of David, was king over Israel and Judah in Jerusalem'. Whatever the source of this verse, we may be sure it was not originally intended to imply a contrast between his reign over Judah and Israel and his reign over foreign countries, and certainly it was not intended to convey the idea that by this time his dominion was limited to Jerusalem city. Not without some clear indication, then, ought we to assume that the editor of Misc. 2 read this midrashic interpretation into the verse.

Yet clear indication there seems to be. First, let us take v. b. There are two things about this verse that suggest that it may have been intended as the first member of a decreasing progression: (1) it describes Solomon's dominion as being 'in all the kingdoms' without further definition or limitation, whereas the other three verses in the series all have limitations of some sort; (2) it stands first in the series, where alone it would fit into a decreasing progression. Its counterpart in the MT, however, has a limitation, thus:

MT 5: 1	Misc. 2 v. b
וּשְׁלֹמֹה הָיָה מוֹשֵׁל	καὶ Σαλωμων ἦν ἄρχων[14]
בְּכָל־הַמַּמְלָכוֹת	ἐν πάσαις ταῖς βασιλείαις
מִן־הַנָּהָר	
אֶרֶץ פְּלִשְׁתִּים	
וְעַד גְּבוּל מִצְרָיִם	
מַגִּשִׁים מִנְחָה	καὶ ἦσαν προσφέροντες δῶρα
וְעֹבְדִים אֶת־שְׁלֹמֹה	καὶ ἐδούλευον τῷ Σαλωμων
כָּל־יְמֵי	πάσας τὰς ἡμέρας
חַיָּיו׃	τῆς ζωῆς αὐτοῦ.

The closeness with which the Greek follows the Hebrew of the MT, where it does follow it, shows that the Greek must have been based on a Hebrew *vorlage* basically the same as the MT. That *vorlage* may, of course, have lacked the limitation; but if so, it cannot be regarded as the original Hebrew: the original Hebrew was presumably not so ludicrous as to claim for Solomon a world-wide dominion without limit. The omission of the limitation, whether by accident or design, is a secondary feature. We may not be able to tell whether it had already been omitted from the LXX's Hebrew *vorlage* or whether the translator dropped it; but the suspicion that the omission was deliberate, is increased when we notice the way in which the Midrash Rabbah[15] quotes this very verse. All it has is *And*

Solomon ruled. One might argue, of course, that this brief quotation of the introductory words of the verse was meant to stand, part for whole, for the complete verse. But this would be very difficult, for the Midrash quite clearly intends the verse to prove that Solomon's dominion was universal: it quotes the verse as the middle term in the following progression.

1. 1 Kings 5: 4, *For he had dominion over all the region on this side the River*, i.e. limited earthly dominion.

2. 1 Kings 5: 1, *And Solomon ruled*.

3. 1 Chron. 29: 23, *Then Solomon sat on the throne of the Lord as king*.

Now this last verse is normally taken by rabbinic exegesis to mean that Solomon reigned over the higher beings (cf. Babylonian Talmud, *Sanhedrin*, 20b). This being so, the middle term between limited earthly dominion and supraterrestrial dominion must be unlimited earthly dominion. But 5: 1 can be adduced in support of the claim that Solomon's dominion was universal only by ignoring or omitting the limitation. And hence the Midrash is found to be treating the limitation in this verse in the same way as v. b of Misc. 2 treats it. It is hardly an accidental coincidence; Misc. 2 too is probably governed by midrashic considerations.

Secondly, take vv. f and k:

v. f. ὅτι ἦν ἄρχων ἐν παντὶ πέραν τοῦ ποταμοῦ ἀπὸ Ραφι ἕως Γάζης, ἐν πᾶσιν τοῖς βασιλεῦσιν πέραν τοῦ ποταμοῦ.

v. k. καὶ ἦν ἄρχων ἐν πᾶσιν τοῖς βασιλεῦσιν ἀπὸ τοῦ ποταμοῦ καὶ ἕως γῆς ἀλλοφύλων καὶ ἕως ὁρίων Αἰγύπτου.

Both of these verses do in fact describe an area of dominion less than that described in v. b; but for our surmise to be true that in Misc. 2 we have a deliberately constructed decreasing progression, we must be able to show that the decrease in vv. f and k has been deliberately contrived. This can be easily done. V. k is nothing but a counterpart of the MT 5: 1, just as v. b is; only in v. b the limitations given in MT 5: 1 have been omitted, while in v. k they have been retained. Could this be accidental? The MT of 5: 1 has two parts:

1. And Solomon was ruling in all the kingdoms from the

river (to) the land of the Philistines and to the frontier of Egypt;

2. they brought tribute and served Solomon all the days of his life.

Of these v. b, as we have just seen (p. 26), has the second part in full, but of the first part it has only 'And Solomon was ruling in all the kingdoms.' V. k, on the other hand, while it lacks the second part, has the first part in full.[16] It is in itself a strange thing that Misc. 2 should have two verses which are both counterparts of MT 5: 1; but when one verse includes the limitations and one omits them, and when the one which omits them is placed first and the one which includes them is placed third, it is very difficult not to conclude that we are in the presence of some very deliberate manipulation.

Thirdly, if our suspicion that vv. f and k are part of a decreasing progression is correct, v. k ought to describe a smaller area of dominion than v. f. As they stand, however, v. f might be taken to describe an area smaller, if anything, than that described in v. k. The phrase in v. f – πέραν τοῦ ποταμοῦ – like its Hebrew counterpart עֵבֶר־הַנָּהָר – is a technical term meaning *west* of the Euphrates, so that when it says ὅτι ἦν ἄρχων ἐν παντὶ πέραν τοῦ ποταμοῦ... ἐν πᾶσιν τοῖς βασιλεῦσιν πέραν τοῦ ποταμοῦ it is saying much the same as v. k, καὶ ἦν ἄρχων ἐν πᾶσιν τοῖς βασιλεῦσιν ἀπὸ τοῦ ποταμοῦ καὶ ἕως γῆς ἀλλο-φύλων καὶ ἕως ὁρίων Αἰγύπτου. But trouble arises with the limitation set in v. f: ἀπὸ Ραφι ἕως Γάζης. The counterpart in the MT at 5: 4 is 'from Tiphsah to Gaza', which makes excellent sense, for Tiphsah, probably identical with Thapsacus, was on the Euphrates and therefore in the extreme east of the area, while Gaza was at the extreme west of the area. But where was Ραφι? It bears little or no resemblance to the Hebrew תִּפְסַח.[17] It could, of course, be a corruption; but the manuscripts show remarkably little variation, Ραφει – Ραφη – Ραφαειν. Mont-gomery suggested[18] that the Egyptian Jewish scribe might have been thinking of Raphia. Geographically this would make sense. The last city on the great military highway from Asia to Egypt, Raphia, whose territory extended to the Egyptian border, would supply an obvious extreme S.-W. limit. But then Gaza is only 15 miles off Raphia, so that to say that Solomon's dominion extended over all Across the River from Raphia to Gaza, not only would give v. f a very much smaller area than v. k, but would in itself be nonsensical. Perhaps, then, we should give up the attempt to identify Ραφι, and assume that v. f indicates a territory as big as, if not bigger than, v. k does.

But the seeming nonsense created (if we accept Montgomery's suggestion) by the nearness of Raphia to Gaza, cannot but recall one of the interpretations advanced in the later rabbinical debate over 1 Kings 5: 4 and the location of Tiphsah and Gaza. One of the several places where this debate is recorded is the Babylonian Talmud, *Megillah*, 11a: 'Rab and Samuel interpreted differently. One said that Tiphsah is at one end of the world and Gaza at the other, and the other said that Tiphsah and Gaza are near one another (and that what is meant is that) as he (Solomon) ruled over Tiphsah and Gaza, so he ruled over all the world.' Perhaps, then, Ραφι, in the phrase ἀπὸ Ραφι ἕως Γάζης in v. f, is not an accidental corruption, but a deliberate exegetical substitution, that puts the better known Raphia for the less known Tiphsah with the intention of arguing that Raphia and Gaza were near one another, and that what the phrase implies is that just as Solomon ruled over Raphia and Gaza, so he ruled over the whole region west of the Euphrates. This cannot, of course, be proved; it must remain only a suspicion. But even if Montgomery's suggestion were accepted, the strange phrase from 'Raphia to Gaza' could not be held to make v. f necessarily indicate a smaller area than v. k; and therefore it would not detract from (if anything, it would add to) the other evidence which suggests that vv. b, f, k and l have been arranged with midrashic care to set out the decreasing stages of Solomon's dominion.

CHAPTER 4

CATEGORIES OF MATERIAL
IN THE MISCELLANIES

Suppose now we have demonstrated that the material in the two miscellanies has been carefully arranged by some editor so as to present two themes, and that in the course of his work the editor has exerted his midrashic skill upon the material to make it yield meanings never originally intended; we still have to ask some further and more basic questions: where did the editor get the material from? what is its relation to the main Greek text? to the MT? to any other Hebrew text tradition? As a first stage towards answering these questions the present chapter sets out to list the various categories of material to be found in the miscellanies, offering probable examples of each with some tentative discussion. The categories, of course, are somewhat arbitrary. Several of the verses are complex and involve material belonging to more than one category. But if we can get the main categories clear in our minds we can then proceed to analyse fully and in detail the more complicated portions.

Editorial addition

We can without hesitation assign to this category v. k of Misc. 1: πλὴν μετὰ τὸ οἰκοδομῆσαι αὐτὸν τὸν οἶκον τοῦ κυρίου καὶ τὸ τεῖχος Ιερουσαλημ κύκλῳ, μετὰ ταῦτα ᾠκοδόμησεν τὰς πόλεις ταύτας.
The two words ἐν πρώτοις in v. c of Misc. 1 also belong to this category. Both items have already been discussed, see pp. 8–9.

Editorial adaptation

Here we ought probably to place v. e of Misc. 1: καὶ ἐποίησεν Σαλωμων τὴν θάλασσαν καὶ τὰ ὑποστηρίγματα καὶ τοὺς λουτῆρας τοὺς μεγάλους καὶ τοὺς στύλους καὶ τὴν κρήνην τῆς αὐλῆς καὶ τὴν θάλασσαν τὴν χαλκῆν.

Compare the main Greek text at 7: 10, 11, 17, 3, and the MT at 7: 23, 24, 30, 15. This verse is not the counterpart of any one verse in the main Greek text or in the MT; it is rather a collection of individual items, most, but not all, of which can be found in different places in the MT and in the main Greek text. But in the process of putting these different items together certain strange features have crept in, which in all probability never stood in any Biblical text tradition at all.

The first thing to notice is that all the items without exception have to do with the court of the temple: the sea, that is the great water-vessel, that stood on twelve oxen, the under-props (ὑποστηρίγματα)[1] of the sea, the ten subsidiary lavers,[2] the two pillars (Jachin and Boaz), and τὴν κρήνην τῆς αὐλῆς, which, whatever it is, belongs explicitly to the court. Next we notice how this list of court items follows the main Greek text and the MT in one large and significant detail: the main Greek text and the MT in their description of the court furniture, 7: 1–37 (MT 7: 13–51), have no mention of the altar of sacrifice although it stood in the court. Likewise this list in v. e has no mention of this altar. Of course the main Greek text and the MT refer to this altar elsewhere; so in fact does Misc. 1, in v. g; but not in v. e – which is significant, since v. e is a freely-composed list.

This said, however, we must turn to two features of v. e that present problems. The first is the repetition τὴν θάλασσαν... καὶ τὴν θάλασσαν τὴν χαλκῆν. This is strange, for there were not two seas in the temple court, one ordinary and one of copper, but only one, and this one was of copper. One's first reaction would be to suppose that the repetition was the result of scribal accident; and this indeed may be the true account of it. But there is no variant: the manuscripts are unanimous in having the first τὴν θάλασσαν. This being so, it is perhaps just possible that the simple term τὴν θάλασσαν had for our editor come to mean something different from τὴν θάλασσαν τὴν χαλκῆν. In Sirach 50: 3 we read that in the course of various repairs to the

temple executed by Simon the High Priest, ἐλατομήθη ἀποδοχεῖον ὑδάτων, λάκκος ὡσεὶ θαλάσσης τὸ περίμετρον. This
object with a perimeter like that of the sea was not, of course,
a laver like the copper sea which Solomon built; it was doubtless a reservoir that formed part of the system for the supply of
water for the temple. Now the temple's water supply is, as
Moses Hadas remarks,[3] a stock theme in post-Biblical descrip-
tions of the temple: Aristeas devotes his sections 88, 89, 90 and
92 to it. Philo the Elder mentions the κρήνη τοῦ ἀρχιερέως and
the ἀποχέτευσις. Tacitus, *Histories* v 12, talking of the temple,
remarks: 'fons perennis aquae, cavati sub terra montes, et
piscinae cisternaeque servandis imbribus'. It might just be,
therefore, that the first τὴν θάλασσαν in v. e was imagined by
the editor of the miscellany to refer to a reservoir like that
built by Simon.

This slight possibility is somewhat increased by the other
difficulty presented by v. e, namely the phrase τὴν κρήνην τῆς
αὐλῆς, the spring of the court. No such spring is mentioned in
the main Greek text or in the MT. Aristeas (89), however,
informs us that there was within the temple area an abundant
natural spring,[4] as well as marvellous underground reservoirs.
Reference to such a spring in v. e, therefore, not only strengthens
our suspicion that our editor is interested in the temple's water-
supply, but it tends to bracket him with those later, post-
Septuagintal writers like Aristeas to whom this water supply
was something of a wonder and a fascination.

There is, moreover, a further indication of the lateness of this
list in v. e, and that is the phrase τοὺς λουτῆρας τοὺς μεγάλους.
These λουτῆρας are presumably the ten lavers set on bases
equipped with wheels, and referred to as λουτῆρας in 7: 17
(MT 7: 30) but elsewhere as χυτροκαύλους (e.g. 7: 24, MT
7: 38). Now these movable lavers were, of course, less imposing
and less important vessels than the sea in association with which
they are normally described. It is rather odd, therefore, to call
them μεγάλους, particularly when they are being mentioned in
the same breath as the sea, which, though in fact a far greater
vessel, is not called great. Certainly neither the main Greek

text nor the MT ever calls these ten lavers 'the great lavers'. The use of this distinguishing epithet suggests a post-Biblical editor whose admiration for the temple was greater than his understanding of the detailed facts.

Now since the presence of the item τὴν κρήνην τῆς αὐλῆς and the repetition of τὴν θάλασσαν do give to v. e a weighty emphasis on the temple's water supply, it might be worth while indulging in one further piece of speculation. For this we must turn to the preceding verse: καὶ ἦν τῷ Σαλωμων ἑβδομήκοντα χιλιάδες αἴροντες ἄρσιν καὶ ὀγδοήκοντα χιλιάδες λατόμων ἐν τῷ ὄρει. As we shall later see (p. 50), this verse duplicates word for word the verse 5: 29 (BM 5: 15) in the main text. The context both in the main Greek text and the MT makes it abundantly clear that these 150,000 men were concerned with the quarrying and haulage of the raw material for building the temple, and that their quarry-work was done in the mountains. But the context of the verse in the miscellany is different. The building of the temple proper has already been mentioned in the first section which concludes in v. c ἐποίησεν καὶ συνετέλεσεν; the verse which follows v. d deals with objects in the temple court and the temple's water supply, none of which would require quarrying in the mountains. Moreover, v. d is very closely linked in subject matter to v. h and yet, instead of placing it, as he could have done, immediately in front of v. h, the editor has chosen to place it in front of v. e. One might wonder, therefore, whether in this context, the mountain in which operated the 'ὀγδοήκοντα χιλιάδες λατόμων ἐν τῷ ὄρει' was in the editor's mind the temple-mount, and whether the quarrying they did was connected in his mind with the first mention of τὴν θάλασσαν in v. e (as distinct from the later mention of τὴν θάλασσαν τὴν χαλκῆν) and understood as the excavation of a reservoir as in Sirach 50: 3 (of the temple) ... ἐλατομήθη[5] ἀποδοχεῖον ὑδάτων, λάκκος ὡσεὶ θαλάσσης τὸ περίμετρον.

We cannot, of course, prove any of this speculation; what we can say with some certainty, however, is that in v. e Biblical items and non-Biblical items have been strung together, not very knowledgeably, and adapted to the editor's purpose.

Two other verses, Misc. 2 v. aˣ and v. l, should probably be listed here. V. l has already been discussed at length, p. 25. V. aˣ, καὶ ἦν ὁ βασιλεὺς Σαλωμων φρόνιμος σφόδρα καὶ σοφός, while resembling in theme verses in the main Greek text and in the MT, has no exact parallel in either. It looks to be an editorial adaptation.[6]

Word for word duplication of the main Greek text

As we have just noted (p. 33), v. d of Misc. 1 is a word for word duplication of the main Greek text at 5: 29 (BM 5: 15). This is interesting, for it seems to show that the miscellanies are not just collections of variants, additions or rejected readings; they have one verse, at least, which repeats exactly what the main text says, and owes its presence in a miscellany presumably because it was necessary to the theme of that miscellany. We may hazard an alternative guess that it stands in the miscellany because it shares with v. h the theme, 'Solomon's servants', and was relegated to the miscellany along with v. h when v. h, for substantial reasons of its own (which we shall later consider, pp. 50ff.), was moved to the miscellany, dragging v. d with it. Even so, it would still leave unanswered the question, why then do not vv. d and h stand together in the miscellany? And the only answer to that would appear to be that its position, even if not its presence, is determined simply by the theme of the miscellany (see above, p. 33).

Variant translation of material in the main Greek text

Verses a and b of Misc. 1 may be taken together. They form a doublet with two verses which stand together in the same order in the main Greek text at 5: 9, 10 (BM 4: 25, 26).

Misc. 1	Main text
2: 35a καὶ ἔδωκεν κύριος	5: 9 καὶ ἔδωκεν κύριος
φρόνησιν τῷ Σ.	φρόνησιν τῷ Σ.
καὶ σοφίαν πολλὴν σφόδρα	καὶ σοφίαν πολλὴν σφόδρα

Misc. 1	Main text
καὶ πλάτος καρδίας	καὶ χύμα καρδίας
ὡς ἡ ἄμμος ἡ παρὰ τὴν	ὡς ἡ ἄμμος ἡ παρὰ τὴν
θάλασσαν	θάλασσαν
35b καὶ ἐπληθύνθη ἡ	καὶ ἐπληθύνθη⁷ Σ.
φρόνησις Σ.	
σφόδρα ὑπὲρ τὴν φρόνησιν	σφόδρα ὑπὲρ τὴν φρόνησιν
πάντων ἀρχαίων υἱῶν καὶ	πάντων ἀρχαίων ἀνθρώπων
	καὶ
ὑπὲρ πάντας φρονίμους	ὑπὲρ πάντας φρονίμους
Αἰγύπτου.	Αἰγύπτου.

The main variants have been underlined. They may conveniently be discussed together, for πλάτος καρδίας is a more literal translation of רֹחַב לֵב than is χύμα καρδίας, and ἀρχαίων υἱῶν is a more literal translation of בְּנֵי קֶדֶם than is ἀρχαίων ἀνθρώπων. The first point to notice is that on both occasions it is the miscellany that has the more literal translation. From this one might easily be tempted to argue that since earlier renderings tend to be freer, and literalistic translations a later phenomenon, the renderings in the main text are original and those in the miscellany were supplied by some later corrector or annotator. And that may be the truth of the matter. But we should at least forewarn ourselves that on other occasions it will be the miscellany that has the freer rendering and the main text the more literal or more correct.

The fact, then, that the miscellany does not take a consistent attitude to the question of free versus literal translation might encourage us to consider other possible origins of the variants. After all, the non-literal χύμα is a very strange word, one might think, to use in connection with καρδίας, and not at all an obvious choice; whereas πλάτος, though literal, makes immediate good sense – 'width of heart', i.e. broad understanding and wide knowledge. In Psalm 118 (119): 32, for instance, תַּרְחִיב לִבִּי is rendered straightforwardly, and literally, ἐπλάτυνας τὴν καρδίαν μου. Is not the literal translation, then, better than the non-literal? Would it even be fair to call it literalistic? A difficulty arises, however, when one tries to fit the phrase to the simile that is used to amplify it, 'like the sand which is by the sea'. Clearly '*width* of heart like the sand...' is unsuitable: the intended comparison is not with the width of the beach, but with the quantity of the sand, or with the infinite number of grains of sand. Χύμα in the sense of 'a large mass or quantity' suits the simile much better, though it remains a strange word to use with καρδία. Or, at least, it seems to us to suit the simile better; but some of the later rabbis were not so sure what the point of the simile was. In Midrash Rabbah,[8] *Ecclesiastes* VII 23, we find:

It is written, And God gave Solomon wisdom...even as the sand that is on the sea-shore (1 Kings v 9). The Rabbis and R. Levi discuss this statement. The Rabbis say: it is written, 'As the sand'. What means 'As the sand'? He was given wisdom equal to that of all Israel. R. Levi said: As the sand is a fence to the sea (that is should not overflow), so was wisdom a fence to Solomon. [See the long discussion of this view in *Pesikta Rabbati*, 14, 8.]

Here are two different interpretations of the simile, one based on the quantity of sand, and the other on its function as a fence. Now, as we have seen above (p. 14), Misc. 2 cites the sand-of-the-sea simile in connection with the number of Judah and Israel: this is clearly the 'quantity' interpretation. But if one accepted R. Levi's somewhat strained interpretation that Solomon's πλάτος καρδίας resembled the beach in that the beach acted like a bulwark, then the width of the beach would by no means be an irrelevant or inappropriate feature. Given an exegetical approach of this kind, πλάτος καρδίας might still be literalistic and secondary, but in this case it would not have been added as a 'correction' of the translation in the main text, nor merely as another translation, but as another, supplementary interpretation helping to screw the very last ounce of meaning out of the Hebrew. Nor would its prime motive have been to bring the Greek nearer to the MT; if another interpretation could be effected by offering a translation which strayed further away from the MT, this kind of exegesis would happily go in that direction as well. We have at least one verse in Misc. 1 that does that very thing, namely v. f^α (see above, p. 19).

On the other hand, the other pair, ἀρχαίων υἱῶν/ἀρχαίων ἀνθρώπων can scarcely be thought to owe their difference to exegetical cunning. Indeed the underlying Hebrew בְּנֵי קֶדֶם offered a glorious opportunity, one might have thought, for the exegetes to differ between the translation οἱ υἱοὶ ἀνατολῶν as in Judges 6: 3, and the translation which we have here, that takes קֶדֶם in the sense ἀρχαιος. The fact that the miscellany and the main text agree over this major matter suggests that υἱῶν instead of ἀνθρώπων is nothing but a translational variant, literalistic and ungainly, with no exegetical implications. And if this is so with this pair, it could be so with the first pair as well.

Midrashic translation

These examples deserve a category of their own to distinguish them from translational variants that are concerned simply with style or with disagreement over the meaning of one and the same Hebrew word. The process by which this so-called midrashic translation arises may be distinguished by the help of an example, that uses English words in the place of Hebrew and Greek. One translator in different places, or several translators in the same place, might legitimately use any one of the synonyms 'boat', 'ship', 'vessel' for the same Hebrew word. But if a translator for exegetical reasons first repointed his Hebrew to read not 'ship' but 'shop' or 'shape' or 'she-ape', the resultant Greek rendering would obviously have a right to be regarded as something different from normal stylistic and other variants.

We have already suggested (see above, p. 22) that v. f^α of Misc. 1 is an example of midrashic translation. The full evidence is:

MT 11: 27   שְׁלֹמֹה בָּנָה אֶת־הַמִּלּוֹא סָגַר אֶת־פֶּרֶץ עִיר דָּוִד אָבִיו

LXX 11: 27 Σαλωμων ᾠκοδόμησεν τὴν ἄκραν· συνέκλεισεν τὸν φραγμὸν τῆς πόλεως Δαυιδ τοῦ πατρὸς αὐτοῦ.

    10: 22^a ...τὴν ἄκραν, τοῦ περιφράξαι τὸν φραγμὸν τῆς πόλεως Δαυιδ.

    2: 35^{fα} καὶ ᾠκοδόμησεν τὴν ἄκραν ἔπαλξιν[9] ἐπ' αὐτῆς· διέκοψεν τὴν πόλιν Δαυιδ.

There is no reason to think the translation at 11: 27 to be anything but the original translation. The phrase in 10: 22[a] seems to be an explanatory gloss; at least, it has nothing to correspond to it in that position in the MT. But its difference in vocabulary περιφράξαι/συνέκλεισεν does not necessarily argue a difference in translator, though it might.[10] On the other hand the differences in 2: 35[fα] are fundamental. I have already given the evidence which suggests that they arose not by accidental mistake[11] but from a deliberate midrashic re-interpretation of the Hebrew; there is no need to repeat it here.

In this category there should also perhaps be placed v. c of Misc. 2 καὶ Σαλωμων ἤρξατο διανοίγειν[12] τὰ δυναστεύματα τοῦ Λιβάνου. At first sight there seems nothing either in the main Greek text or in the MT to correspond to this verse. A clue to its possible origin is provided by the following verse, v. d, καὶ αὐτὸς ᾠκοδόμησεν τὴν Θερμαι ἐν τῇ ἐρήμῳ. This verse, as we have already seen (p. 16), has its counterpart in the MT at 9: 15–19 and in the main Greek text at 10: 22[a] (BM 10: 23, 24), a context that is relating the cities which Solomon built. The full evidence is:[13]

Misc. 1 v. 35[i]	MT 9: 15	10: 22[a]
τὴν Ασσουρ	וְאֶת־חָצֹר	καὶ τὴν Ασσουρ
καὶ τὴν Μαγδω	וְאֶת־מְגִדּוֹ	καὶ τὴν Μαγδαν
καὶ τὴν Γαζερ	וְאֶת־גָּזֶר	καὶ τὴν Γαζερ

But at this point the MT has a long explanation: 'Pharaoh king of Egypt had gone up, and taken Gezer, and burnt it with fire, and slain the Canaanites that dwelt in the city, and given it for a portion unto his daughter, Solomon's wife. And Solomon built Gezer...' After this explanation it proceeds with the list of cities built by Solomon. The Greek 2: 35[i] lacks this explanation altogether; the main Greek text lacks it in this context, but has it at 5: 14[a and b] (BM 4: 32, 33); both proceed in our present contexts simply with the list of cities:

v. 35[i]	MT 9: 17[b], 18	10: 22[a]
καὶ τὴν Βαιθωρων	וְאֶת־בֵּית חֹרֹן	καὶ τὴν Βαιθωρων
τὴν ἐπάνω	תַּחְתּוֹן	τὴν ἀνωτέρω

v. 35[i]	MT 9: 17[b], 18	10: 22[a]
καὶ τὰ Βααλαθ	וְאֶת־בַּעֲלָת	—
(Misc. 2 v. d)		
καὶ αὐτὸς ᾠκοδό-μησεν	וְאֶת־תָּמֹר[14]	καὶ τὴν Ιεθερμαθ
τὴν Θερμαι ἐν τῇ ἐρήμῳ	בַּמִּדְבָּר בָּאָרֶץ	

Now in the MT the next verse, 9: 19, continues the list of cities with: 'and all the store cities that Solomon had, and the cities for his chariots, and the cities for his horsemen, and that which Solomon desired to build for his pleasure in Jerusalem, and in Lebanon, and in all the land of his dominion'. In the main Greek text 'and in Lebanon' is missing from the last part of this verse. Perhaps this then is the source of τοῦ Λιβάνου in Misc. 2 v. c.

That still leaves καὶ Σαλωμων ἤρξατο διανοίγειν τὰ δυναστεύματα to be accounted for. Now the main Greek text has likewise no counterpart for וְאֶת־בַּעֲלָת and Montgomery[15] has made the interesting suggestion that τὰ δυναστεύματα represents בעלת read as בעלות and that (δι)ανοίγειν goes back to a Hebrew bḳʿ 'to breach, capture'.[16] On this interpretation δυναστεύματα would have to be given some such meaning as 'fortresses'.

The probability of Montgomery's suggestion is increased by the fact that Misc. 1's counterpart of ואת־בעלת is the only name to have its article in the plural τὰ Βααλαθ, which shows that its *vorlage* had been read as a plural. The interesting thing is that if Montgomery's suggestion is correct, then Misc. 1 and Misc. 2 between them have two interpretations of ואת־בעלת, one a transliteration, one a translation.

But διανοίγειν τὰ δυναστεύματα is, to say the least of it, a very literalistic translation. δυνάστευμα is not, according to Liddell and Scott, citable as meaning 'fortress'; indeed they hazard the guess for our verse 'natural resources'. The noun is not elsewhere used in the LXX; but the verb δυναστεύω, and the nouns δυναστεία, δυνάστης occur very many times, and nowhere else do they represent √בעל. Moreover, וְאֶת־בַּעֲלָת stands, in the MT at least, at quite a distance from וּבַלְּבָנוֹן,

separated by the words: 'and Tamar-in-the-Steppe in the land
and all the store cities which Solomon had and the cities for his
chariots and the cities for his horsemen, and that which Solomon
desired to build in Jerusalem and in Lebanon and in all the land
of his dominion'. To isolate Lebanon from all this and put it
together with Baalath, and to supply a couple of verbs 'began
to open' seems a very arbitrary procedure, whether done by
some Hebrew text (unless it were a free composition bearing no
relation to the MT) or by a translator. Add to this the mistranslation of Baalath in Misc. 2 whereas Misc. 1 has a correct
transliteration, and one gets the impression once more that one
is being offered, not simply a variant translation, but a fanciful
midrashic alternative interpretation.[17]

Material lacking in the main Greek text but present in the MT

One simple example of this will be sufficient here: Misc. 2 v. a$^\beta$,
καὶ Ιουδα καὶ Ισραηλ πολλοὶ σφόδρα ὡς ἡ ἄμμος ἡ ἐπὶ τῆς
θαλάσσης εἰς πλῆθος, ἐσθίοντες καὶ πίνοντες καὶ χαίροντες.
Apart from the word σφόδρα this is an exact equivalent of
MT 4: 20; the main Greek text has no counterpart. The facts,
then, are simple.

Now it is temptingly easy to explain this situation by saying
that the main Greek text was based on a non-MT Hebrew text
which lacked this verse, and the presence of the verse in the
miscellany is the work of a reviser who wished to add to the
main text the extra details which he found in the MT. Actually
the situation is much more complicated than that.

First we may notice that if v. a$^\beta$ is matched by MT 4: 20, the
next verse, v. b, is also matched by the next verse in the MT,
5: 1. Now v. b has no counterpart at all in the main Greek text,
but at the same time it does not conform to the MT either. It
omits a long phrase, and the omission, as we have already seen
(p. 26), is very significant for the theme of the miscellany.
Conformity, then, to the MT may have determined the *order*
of vv. a$^\beta$ and b, but not the *content* of v. b.

Secondly, if we examine the larger context from which v. a$^\beta$

comes, both in the main Greek text and in the MT, we find that the Greek differs from the MT in a number of places both in order and content.

	Main Greek text[18]			MT
4: 1–6	Solomon's princes		4: 1–6	Solomon's princes
4: 7–19	Solomon's victualling officers.		4: 7–19	Solomon's victualling officers
	omitted by main text: but = Misc. 2 v. a$^\beta$		4: 20	Judah and Israel were many as the sand which is by the sea in multitude eating and drinking and making merry.
			5: 1a	And Solomon ruled over all the kingdoms
	omitted by main text here but 1a and 1c = Misc. 2 v. b, and the main text at 10: 26^a		b	from the River to the land of the Philistines and to the border of Egypt:
	has an equivalent of 1a and 1b		c	they brought him presents and served Solomon all the days of his life.
5: 1	And the officers provided victual…and barley and chaff for horses…			see below 5: 7–8
5: 2–3	Solomon's daily provision		5: 2–3	Solomon's daily provision
5: 4a	For he had dominion across the River		5: 4a	For he had dominion over all across the River
b	omitted by main text[19] but = Misc. 2 v. f$^\beta$		b	from Tiphsah even to Gaza over all the kings across the River:
c	and he had peace on all sides round about.		c	and he had peace on all sides round about him.

Main Greek Text			MT
omitted by main text but = Misc. 2 v. g$^\beta$		5: 5	And Judah and Israel dwelt safely...all the days of Solomon.
omitted from main text here, but near equivalent at 10: 26 (BM 29) and at Misc. 2 v. i.		5: 6	And Solomon had 40,000 stalls of horses for his chariots and 12,000 horsemen.
see above at 5: 1		5: 7–8	And those officers provided victual...and barley and chaff for horses...
5: 9–11	Solomon's superlative wisdom	5: 9–11	Solomon's superlative wisdom
5: 12–13	Solomon's wise sayings	5: 12–13	Solomon's wise sayings
5: 14a	All come to hear his wisdom	5: 14	All come to hear his wisdom.
b	He received presents from all the kings of the earth, as many as heard his wisdom.		nothing here; but compare 5: 1c above.

Now it is at once obvious that the arrangement in the main Greek text is carefully devised to present its material in an uninterrupted, logical order. This is particularly marked if one compares its passage 4: 1–5: 4 with the MT 4: 1–5: 8. The Greek has the princes, then the officers, whose job it was to provide victuals (4: 7), then, without interruption the statement (5: 1) that they did in fact provide the victuals, followed immediately (5: 2–3) by a list of the victuals provided, and finally the explanation (5: 4) why the victualling was so abundant. Compared with this neat arrangement, that of the MT seems clumsy: the verses 4: 20 and 5: 1 seem to interrupt the theme of Solomon's victualling officers, and 5: 7–8 seem to have got misplaced. Maybe the MT's order and content are secondary. But our point at the moment is to discover what relation the material in the miscellanies bears to this situation. It is, of course, true that they supply most of the material which is in the MT but which is lacking in the main Greek text – this one can see from the list above. But they do far more, which is not deducible from the list above: they duplicate, with significant variants in translation, a good deal of what the main Greek text does supply. Misc. 2 v. h duplicates the list of princes (4: 1–6) – the differences are many and large. Misc. 2 v. e duplicates, with a significant difference, Solomon's daily provision (5: 2–3). Misc. 2 v. i duplicates the item on horses at 10: 26, and v. b duplicates the first part of 10: 26[a]. Misc. 2 v. f[α] duplicates 5: 4a and v. g[α] duplicates 5: 4c. It is clearly insufficient to think of the miscellanies as merely trying to supply that much of the MT that was lacking in the main Greek text, for they do much more than this. On the other hand, though they do more than this, they do not attempt themselves to reproduce the MT fully either in quantity or order: they lack the long list of the victualling officers (4: 7–19), the statement on the performance of those officers (5: 7–8) and an equivalent for 5: 1b.[20]

What then are the miscellanies trying to do? To understand this we shall obviously need to examine carefully the differences between the miscellanies and the main Greek text in passages in which the miscellanies duplicate the main Greek text. In other words we must look very closely at material which comes under the already mentioned category, Variant Translation. Before we do that, however, there is another category with which we should acquaint ourselves.

Material based on a Hebrew text different from the MT of 1 Kings

We have already had occasion to notice (p. 27) that v. b and v. k of Misc. 2 seem both to be counterparts of MT 5: 1, and that neither of them seems to have an exact counterpart in the main Greek text. But now we must make our observations more precise. Here are v. b and v. k compared with the MT of 1 Kings 5: 1.

MT 5:1	v. b	v. k
וּשְׁלֹמֹה הָיָה מוֹשֵׁל	καὶ Σ. ἦν ἄρχων	καὶ ἦν ἄρχων
בְּכָל־הַמַּמְלָכוֹת	ἐν πάσαις ταῖς βασι-λείαις	ἐν πᾶσιν τοῖς βασι-λεῦσιν

43

MT 5:1 v. b v. k

מִן־הַנָּהָר — ἀπὸ τοῦ ποταμοῦ

אֶרֶץ פְּלִשְׁתִּים — καὶ ἕως γῆς ἀλλοφύ-λων

וְעַד גְּבוּל מִצְרָיִם — καὶ ἕως ὁρίων Αἰγύπτου

מַעֲשִׂים מִנְחָה — καὶ ἦσαν προσφέ-ροντες δῶρα

וְעֹבְדִים אֶת־שׁ" — καὶ ἐδούλευον τῷ Σ.

כָּל־יְמֵי — πάσας τὰς ἡμέρας

חַיָּיו — τῆς ζωῆς αὐτοῦ.

In spite of the general similarity, there are in the section common to MT 5: 1 and v. k some tell-tale differences: v. k has no 'Solomon' whereas the MT and v. b have; v. k has 'kings', whereas the MT and v. b have 'kingdoms'; and v. k has καὶ ἕως before γῆς while the MT has no וְעַד before אֶרֶץ. So v. k is not an *exact* counterpart of MT 1 Kings 5: 1. But there is a Hebrew text which matches v. k exactly, and that is MT 2 Chron. 9: 26:

וַיְהִי מוֹשֵׁל בְּכָל־הַמְּלָכִים — καὶ ἦν ἄρχων ἐν πᾶσιν τοῖς βασι-λεῦσιν

מִן־הַנָּהָר — ἀπὸ τοῦ ποταμοῦ

וְעַד אֶרֶץ פְּלִשְׁתִּים — καὶ ἕως γῆς ἀλλοφύλων

וְעַד גְּבוּל מִצְרָיִם: — καὶ ἕως ὁρίων Αἰγύπτου.

It would seem, then, that while v. b is based on the MT of 1 Kings 5: 1, v. k is based on a Hebrew text of 1 Kings 5: 1 that differed from the MT of Kings and agreed with the MT of Chronicles. On this showing one can easily explain why v. b and v. k apparently duplicate the translation of 5: 1: they are translations of slightly different text-traditions.

This, however, still leaves a further question to be answered: why do both of these verses, duplicating the same material, though in slightly different text-forms, stand in the miscellany, with seemingly no counterpart in the main Greek text? Why was

44

not one of the duplicates put in the main text? The answer is
that the main Greek text does in fact have a counterpart to
vv. b and k, only it stands not at 5: 1 but at 10: 26ᵃ (BM 10: 30);
in this position it has nothing to correspond to it in the MT of
1 Kings. The curious thing is, however, that this translation at
10: 26ᵃ proves to be based on a Hebrew text of the same type
as v. k and 2 Chron. 9: 26; and what is more it agrees word for
word with the translation of 2 Chron. 9: 26 given by 2 Paralipomena 9: 26. Here are the three translations for comparison:

3 Reigns 2: 46ᵏ	3 Reigns 10: 26ᵃ	2 Paralip. 9: 26
καὶ ἦν ἄρχων ἐν	καὶ ἦν ἡγούμενος	καὶ ἦν ἡγούμενος
πᾶσιν	πάντων	πάντων
τοῖς βασιλεῦσιν	τῶν βασιλέων	τῶν βασιλέων
ἀπὸ τοῦ ποταμοῦ	ἀπὸ τοῦ ποταμοῦ	ἀπὸ τοῦ ποταμοῦ
καὶ ἕως γῆς ἀλλο-	καὶ ἕως γῆς ἀλλο-	καὶ ἕως γῆς αλλο-
φύλων	φύλων	φύλων
καὶ ἕως ὁρίων	καὶ ἕως ὁρίων²¹	καὶ ἕως ὁρίων²²
Αἰγύπτου.	Αἰγύπτου.	Αἰγύπτου.

The difference between v. k on the one hand and the other
two translations on the other is small: ἄρχων ἐν πᾶσιν τοῖς
βασιλεῦσιν/ἡγούμενος πάντων τῶν βασιλέων. But ἄρχων ἐν +
Dative is not only a more literal translation of "משל ב, it is an
insufferable literalism. "משל ב means 'to rule over', but ἄρχων
ἐν can only mean 'to rule among' or 'to be ruler in'; so that
ἦν ἄρχων ἐν τοῖς βασιλεῦσιν would to a Greek mean 'he was
ruler among the kings'.

So then, v. k of Misc. 2 is a literalistic translation compared
with the main Greek text at 10: 26ᵃ. Shall we then say that
10:26ᵃ because it is freer must be the original Greek translation
and v. k because it is literalistic must be a later addition? Or
shall we say that v. k, because it is crude, is Old Greek, which
has been banished to the miscellany by a later correction, in
more polished Greek, at 10: 26ᵃ?

Two observations may help to answer these questions. First,
Misc. 2 is everywhere consistent in its usage: its verses b, f
and k all describe the extent of Solomon's dominion and all use

ἄρχων not ἡγούμενος. The main Greek text is not so consistent:
at 5: 4 (BM 4: 24) it uses ἄρχων, at 10: 26[a], as we have seen,
ἡγούμενος. More significantly, when the main text uses ἄρχων
at 5: 4, it has simply ἦν ἄρχων πέραν τοῦ ποταμοῦ as
distinct from Misc. 2 v. f ἦν ἄρχων ἐν παντὶ πέραν τοῦ ποταμοῦ.
At 5: 4 only Ax boc₂e₂ Arm. Syr. have ἐν παντὶ πέραν which
doubtless is an Origenic addition, the literalism of which
contrasts with the freer earlier Greek. This then would seem to
suggest that the literalism ἄρχων ἐν in Misc. 2 indicates that
the material in Misc. 2 is late.

The second observation is one about which I have written at
length elsewhere;[23] I need only summarise the argument there
given. Just as v. k of Misc. 2 is a counterpart of the Hebrew
1 Kings 5: 1, so v. i is a counterpart of the Hebrew of 1 Kings
5: 6 (and, what is more, of the MT of this passage):

MT 1 Kings 5: 6	Misc. 2 v. i
וַיְהִי לִשְׁלֹמֹה	καὶ ἦσαν τῷ Σαλωμων
אַרְבָּעִים אֶלֶף	τεσσαράκοντα χιλιάδες
אָרוֹת סוּסִים	τοκάδες ἵπποι[24]
לְמֶרְכָּבוֹ	εἰς ἅρματα
וּשְׁנֵים־עָשָׂר אֶלֶף	καὶ δώδεκα χιλιάδες
פָּרָשִׁים	ἱππέων.

Once again the main Greek text has a counterpart of this, but
not in ch. 5 where it would be expected, but at 10: 26 (first
half).[25] Moreover, the translation given at 10: 26 differs from
that in v. i and matches word for word the translation given in
2 Paralipomena 9: 25a.

Misc. 2 v. i	3 Reigns 10: 26	2 Paralipomena 9: 25
καὶ ἦσαν τῷ Σ.	καὶ ἦσαν τῷ Σ.	καὶ ἦσαν τῷ Σ.
τεσσαράκοντα	τέσσαρες	τέσσαρες
χιλιάδες	χιλιάδες	χιλιάδες
τοκάδες ἵπποι	θήλειαι ἵπποι	θήλειαι ἵπποι
εἰς ἅρματα	εἰς ἅρματα	εἰς ἅρματα
καὶ δώδεκα	καὶ δώδεκα	καὶ δώδεκα
χιλιάδες ἱππέων.	χιλιάδες ἱππέων.	χιλιάδες ἱππέων.

Now while v. i and the other two differ over the translation τοκάδες ἵπποι/θήλειαι ἵπποι, the difference is not perhaps so remarkable as the fact that they all take the underlying Hebrew to mean 'brood mares' when in fact it means 'stalls for horses'. On the other hand, the difference in numbers, 40,000/4,000 is significant; for while the 40,000 brood mares of v. i agrees with the MT of 1 Kings 5: 4, and the 4,000 brood mares of 2 Paralip. 9: 25 agrees with the MT of 2 Chron. 9: 25, the 4,000 brood mares of 3 Reigns 10: 26 does not agree with the MT of 1 Kings 10: 26, which has 1,400 chariots. What happened seems to be this: the 4,000 of 3 Reigns 10: 26 is a correction[26] of the 40,000 given by the MT of 1 Kings 5: 4 (and hence by 2 Misc. v. i), but the correction has somehow got misplaced. The MT of 1 Kings 10: 26 is not the counterpart of 2 Chron. 9: 25 but of 2 Chron. 1: 14. Moreover the MT of 1 Kings 10: 26 did not need to be 'corrected': it agrees exactly with 2 Chron. 1: 14. The MT of 1 Kings 5: 4, on the other hand, did need 'correction' to bring it into line with 2 Chron. 9: 25; but the main Greek text has taken the 'correct' reading of 2 Chron. 9: 25, copying word for word the Greek translation of the whole verse (2 Paralipomena 9: 25), and applied it to the wrong place – ch. 10, instead of ch. 5, of 3 Reigns.[27]

But why should the main Greek text do such a curious thing? Why did it not put the correction in ch. 5 where it belonged? The reason would seem to be that that context in the main Greek text has, as we have already seen (p. 42), been carefully arranged according to a very neat plan which allows no room for the item of Solomon's brood mares (or horse-stalls). Of course, this arrangement could be based on some non-MT Hebrew which itself lacked the item of horses with its faulty number; on the other hand the 'correction' in the main Greek text at 10: 26 seems to presume some knowledge of the MT's faulty number at 5: 4. That the main Greek text, as it stands, does not represent the original Hebrew, however, is shown by the following comparison: of the two items, horse-stalls and chariots, the MT of 1 Kings has both (5: 4 and 10: 26); the MT of 2 Chron. has both (9: 25 and 1: 14); the Greek of

2 Paralipomena has both (9: 25 and 1: 14, though it translates 'horse-stalls' by 'brood mares'); but the main Greek text of 3 Reigns has only stalls (10: 26 – it too calls them 'brood mares') and it has them in the wrong place.

What of Misc. 2? Its v. i agrees with the MT of 1 Kings 5: 4 in every respect including its faulty number. Maybe it was the original Greek translation and once stood in the main Greek text in ch. 5, being banished to the miscellany when the context of ch. 5 was re-arranged to stand in its present meticulous order. Or, if the present order and content of ch. 5 represent the original translation, v. i of Misc. 2 may be a later attempt based on the MT to add what was missing. But in deciding this issue – if it can be decided – the following facts should be borne in mind. First, v. k, as we have seen (p. 44) is not based on the MT of 1 Kings but on another Hebrew text of 1 Kings that agrees with the MT of 2 Chronicles, or else on the MT of 2 Chronicles itself. Secondly, vv. b, e, f, g, i and k all have counterparts in the MT of 1 Kings 5, but their order is different:

Misc. 2		MT 1 Kings 5
v. b	=	v. 1
v. e	=	vv. 2, 3
vv. f, g	=	vv. 4, 5
v. i	=	v. 6
v. k	=	v. 1

Notice particularly vv. i and k; they show no consuming desire to reproduce the MT. At the same time their order agrees with that of the main Greek text and that of 2 Paralipomena:

v. i = main text 10: 26 (first half) = 2 Paralip. 9: 25a
v. k = main text 10: 26^a = 2 Paralip. 9: 26.

Perhaps the order of vv. i and k was even determined by the order of the main Greek text. But the item in the main text at 10: 26 which 'corrects' the faulty number given by v. i is itself faultily placed, as we have seen. It is difficult to resist the conclusion that both v. i and 10: 26 owe their position to one and the same operation which was not designed to make the main text conform to the MT but to record all variants, to give preference in the main text to those that were deemed to be correct, perhaps tacitly thereby to 'correct' the others even if it meant going against the MT, but not to discard them, rather to preserve them in the miscellanies and to make some exegetical profit out of them in their own right.

CHAPTER 5

SOME SPECIAL CASES

Armed with the knowledge that the basic material in the miscellanies can be of several different kinds we must now attempt to analyse in detail some of the more complex portions of it.

(I) THE CASE OF SOLOMON'S OFFICERS

From Misc. 1

v. d. καὶ ἦν τῷ Σαλωμων ἑβδομήκοντα χιλιάδες αἴροντες ἄρσιν καὶ ὀγδοήκοντα χιλιάδες λατόμων ἐν τῷ ὄρει.

v. h. καὶ οὗτοι οἱ ἄρχοντες οἱ καθεσταμένοι ἐπὶ τὰ ἔργα τοῦ Σαλωμων τρεῖς χιλιάδες καὶ ἑξακόσιοι ἐπιστάται τοῦ λαοῦ τῶν ποιούντων τὰ ἔργα.

From the main Greek text

The main text has nowhere a strict counterpart of v. h; but at 5: 29 (BM: 15) it has a word for word duplicate of v. d, which it follows in v. 30 with material that is very relevant to v. h.

5: 29. καὶ ἦν τῷ Σαλωμων ἑβδομήκοντα χιλιάδες αἴροντες ἄρσιν καὶ ὀγδοήκοντα χιλιάδες λατόμων ἐν τῷ ὄρει.

5: 30. χωρὶς ἀρχόντων τῶν καθεσταμένων ἐπὶ τῶν ἔργων τῶν Σαλωμων, τρεῖς χιλιάδες καὶ ἑξακόσιοι ἐπιστάται οἱ ποιοῦντες τὰ ἔργα.

The only question that v. d raises is why it should exist in the miscellany at all seeing it is a word for word duplicate of the main Greek text at 5: 29. Quite clearly it was not designed to fill up that much of the MT that was missing in the main Greek text: the main text, no less than v. d, accurately represents the MT. It would seem that it exists in the miscellany simply because it is connected in subject matter with v. h, about which there are many questions.

Now there is no difficulty in locating the counterpart of v. h in the MT. V. h is the last of three items in Misc. 1 that all stand together and all have a counterpart in the MT 9: 23–5. Here are vv. f$^{\beta\gamma}$, g, h of Misc. 1:

35$^{f(\beta\gamma)}$ οὕτως θυγάτηρ Φαραω ἀνέβαινεν ἐκ τῆς πόλεως Δαυιδ εἰς τὸν οἶκον αὐτῆς, ὃν ᾠκοδόμησεν αὐτῇ· τότε ᾠκοδόμησεν τὴν ἄκραν.

35^{g} καὶ Σαλωμων ἀνέφερεν τρεῖς ἐν τῷ ἐνιαυτῷ ὁλοκαυτώσεις καὶ εἰρηνικὰς ἐπὶ τὸ θυσιαστήριον, ὃ ᾠκοδόμησεν τῷ κυρίῳ, καὶ ἐθυμία ἐνώπιον κυρίου. καὶ συνετέλεσεν τὸν οἶκον.

35^{h} καὶ οὗτοι οἱ ἄρχοντες οἱ καθεσταμένοι ἐπὶ τὰ ἔργα τοῦ Σαλωμων· τρεῖς χιλιάδες καὶ ἑξακόσιοι ἐπιστάται τοῦ λαοῦ τῶν ποιούντων τὰ ἔργα.

Here there are three main items:

1. Pharaoh's daughter.
2. Solomon's offerings.
3. Solomon's officers.

Here is the MT of 1 Kings 9: 23, 24, 25.

23 These were the chief officers that were over Solomon's work, five hundred and fifty, which bare rule over the people that wrought in the work.

24 But Pharaoh's daughter came up out of the city of David unto her house which Solomon had built for her: then did he build Millo.

25 And three times in a year did Solomon offer burnt offerings and peace offerings upon the altar which he built unto the LORD, burning incense (therewith) before the LORD. So he finished the house.

The MT, then, has the same three items as Misc. 1, only Misc. 1 has them in a different order, so that v. h, which is the counterpart of MT 9: 23, comes at the end and not the beginning.[1]

Next we look at the main Greek text to find out what it has done with these three items. We discover that they are caught up in a difference of arrangement that involves not only them but the whole paragraph in the MT in which their counterparts stand. The Greek's counterparts of that paragraph (MT 9: 15–26) are as follows:

MT	Main Greek text[2]	Misc. 1	Misc. 2
9: 15a	10: 22a		
9: 15b	10: 22a	v. i	
9: 16 ⎱ 9: 17a ⎰	4: 14b		
9: 17b	10: 22a		
9: 18	10: 22a		v. d
9: 19	10: 22a		v. c
9: 20–2	10: 22b–c		
9: 23		v. h	
9: 24	9: 9a	v. f$^{\beta\gamma}$	
9: 25		v. g	

I have elsewhere[3] argued at length that the arrangement of the material in the main Greek text is secondary and that it has been devised for the easily discernible midrashic purpose of white-washing Solomon's character. Be that as it may, it is the fact that for some reason the main Greek text has no counterpart of MT 9: 23, while Misc. 1 has a counterpart. This leads us naturally to ask whether the original intention behind the inclusion of v. h in Misc. 1 was to add that much of the MT as was missing in the main text. Clearly the question should not be asked concerning v. h by itself, but in conjunction with vv. f$^{\beta\gamma}$ and g. And even at first sight the answer seems to be no. First there is the difference in order between these verses and the MT, though that could be a later feature imposed upon the verses by the editor of the miscellany. More significant is the fact that neither v. h nor v. g agrees with the MT in detail; and v. f$^{\beta\gamma}$, which comes nearest to reproducing the MT, *has* a counterpart in the main Greek text. With vv. f$^{\beta\gamma}$ and g we will deal in detail later; for the moment we must concentrate on v. h.

Here then is v. h compared with the MT verse of which it is the counterpart:

MT 9: 23	Misc. 1 v. h
אֵלֶּה שָׂרֵי	καὶ οὗτοι οἱ ἄρχοντες
הַנִּצָּבִים	οἱ καθεσταμένοι
אֲשֶׁר	
עַל־הַמְּלָאכָה	ἐπὶ τὰ ἔργα
לִשְׁלֹמֹה	τοῦ Σαλωμων
חֲמִשִּׁים וַחֲמֵשׁ מֵאוֹת	τρεῖς χιλιάδες καὶ ἑξακόσιοι
הָרֹדִים בָּעָם	ἐπιστάται τοῦ λαοῦ
הָעֹשִׂים בַּמְּלָאכָה׃	τῶν ποιούντων τὰ ἔργα.

We notice at once the very big difference in number between 550 and 1,360; it is hardly likely to be due to a misreading of a Hebrew *vorlage* or to a subsequent scribal error. We should also notice that the MT begins 'These were the captains of those appointed who were over the work', whereas the Greek reads 'And these were the captains who were appointed over the works'; in other words, the MT has two classes – 'captains' and 'those appointed', i.e. 'foremen'; the Greek has only one – 'captains who were appointed'. Clearly v. h is not trying to follow the MT too closely. What text, if any, is it following?

Our first clue is that its number, 3,600, occurs twice in 2 Chronicles. We have already seen (p. 45) that the Greek Chronicles seems to have exerted some influence on the Greek main text at 10: 26a, and that v. k of Misc. 2 is based on a Hebrew text which coincides with the Hebrew text of 2 Chron. 9: 26. Perhaps, then, a study of 2 Chronicles will help elucidate our problem on this occasion as well.

In 2 Chron. 2: 16–17 (EVV 2: 17–18) there is mentioned a group of 153,600 workers. They are explicitly described as 'the strangers that were in the land', i.e. they were the *Gentile* levy. The total, 153,600, is made up as follows:

1. 70,000 bearers of burdens
2. 80,000 hewers in the mountains
3. 3,600 foremen to set the people awork.

We should notice the figure 3,600 and the fact that these 3,600 were Gentile foremen of some sort. The Greek calls them ἐργοδιῶκται.[4]

In 2 Chron. 2: 1 (MT, LXX = EVV 2: 2) we find mentioned a labour force made up as follows:

70,000 bearers of burdens
80,000 hewers in the mountains
3,600 foremen.

This seems to be the same force as the one we have just considered in 2: 16–17. If so, though it is not explicitly stated, it is the Gentile levy. This time the 3,600 Gentile foremen are called in the Greek ἐπιστάται.

But 2 Chronicles has another passage, 8: 10, which talks of another, superficially similar, group of men, but explicitly says that they were not Gentiles but Israelites. The previous verses in this context, 7 and 8, have been speaking of the Gentile nations left in the land of whom Solomon raised a levy. But then vv. 9 and 10 continue: 'But of the children of Israel did Solomon make no servants for his work; but they were men of war, and chief of his captains, and rulers of his chariots and of his horsemen. And these were the chief officers of king Solomon, even two hundred-and-fifty, that bare rule over the people.' Context, then, and the different number, 250, make it clear that these chief officers, although described in the Greek as ἐργοδιωκτοῦντες ἐν τῷ λαῷ, were a quite different group from the 3,600 overseers whom the Greek of 2 Chron. describes as ἐργοδιώκτας ἐπὶ τὸν λαόν in 2: 17, and as ἐπιστάται in 2: 2. The 3,600 are Gentile foremen; the 250 are Israelite officers. The account in Chronicles, then, is clear and unconfused; trouble begins only when we compare it with the MT and the Greek of Kings.

Let us take the MT first. 1 Kings 9: 23 is the counterpart of 2 Chron. 8: 10, and it will be worth citing the larger context to show that not only these two verses but also their contexts are basically the same:

1 Kings 9: 20–3		2 Chron. 8: 7–10
20 As for all the people that were left of the Amorites, the Hittites, the Perizzites, the Hi-	7	As for all the people that wer‹ left of the Hittites, and th‹ Amorites, and the Perizzites

1 Kings 9:20–3

vites, and the Jebusites, which
were not of the children of
21 Israel; their children that were
left after them in the land,
whom the children of Israel
were not able utterly to
destroy, of them did Solomon
raise a levy of bondservants,
22 unto this day. But of the
children of Israel did Solomon make no bondservants;
but they were the men of war,
and his servants, and his
princes, and his captains, and
rulers of his chariots and of
23 his horsemen. These were the
chief officers that were over
Solomon's work, five hundred
and fifty, which bare rule
over the people that wrought
in the work.

2 Chron. 8:7–10

and the Hivites, and the Jebu-
8 sites, which were not of
Israel; of their children that
were left after them in the
land, whom the children of
Israel consumed not, of them
did Solomon raise a levy unto
9 this day. But of the children
of Israel did Solomon make
no servants for his work; but
they were men of war, and
chief of his captains, and
rulers of his chariots and of
10 his horsemen. And these were
the chief officers of king
Solomon, even two hundred
and fifty, that bare rule over
the people.

The two passages disagree over the number of the chief officers: Kings says 550, Chronicles 250. But this disagreement may well be the result of scribal error, for both passages are clearly speaking about the same group of men, the Israelite officers; certainly there is no confusion with the 3,600 Gentile foremen.

Now we look at the Greek. The counterpart of MT 9: 23 is, as we have demonstrated (p. 53), v. h of Misc. 1. It will be instructive to compare v. h with the MT of 9: 23 and also with the MT of 2 Chron. 8: 10 and its Greek translation.

	MT 1 Kings 9: 23	Misc. 1 v. h	2 Chron. 8: 10	2 Paralip. 8: 10
1.	אֵלֶּה	καὶ οὗτοι	וְאֵלֶּה	καὶ οὗτοι
2.	שָׂרֵי	οἱ ἄρχοντες	שָׂרֵי	ἄρχοντες

	MT 1 Kings 9: 23	Misc. 1 v. h	2 Chron. 8: 10	2 Paralip. 8: 10
3.	הַנִּצָּבִים	οἱ καθεσταμένοι	⁵הַנִּצִּיבִים	τῶν προστατῶν
4.	אֲשֶׁר עַל־הַמְּלָאכָה	ἐπὶ τὰ ἔργα	אֲשֶׁר־לַמֶּלֶךְ	βασιλέως
5.	לִשְׁלֹמֹה	τοῦ Σαλωμων	שְׁלֹמֹה	Σαλωμων
6.	חֲמִשִּׁים	τρεῖς χιλιάδες	חֲמִשִּׁים	πεντήκοντα
7.	וַחֲמֵשׁ מֵאוֹת	καὶ ἑξακόσιοι	וּמָאתַיִם	καὶ διακόσιοι
8.	הָרֹדִים	ἐπιστάται	הָרֹדִים	ἐργοδιωκτοῦντες
9.	בָּעָם	τοῦ λαοῦ	בָּעָם	ἐν τῷ λαῷ.
10.	הָעֹשִׂים	τῶν ποιούντων		
11.	בַּמְּלָאכָה	τὰ ἔργα.		

Certain things are at once obvious. The Greek of 2 Paralipomena 8: 10 is a very close reproduction of the MT of 2 Chronicles 8: 10. Similarly the Greek of Misc. 1 v. h follows the MT of 1 Kings in details in which the MT of 1 Kings differs from the MT of 2 Chronicles: note particularly items 4–5 and 10–11. On the other hand v. h does not reproduce the MT of 1 Kings as faithfully as 2 Paralipomena reproduces the MT of 2 Chronicles. In the small matter of item 9, τοῦ λαοῦ is a less literal translation of בָּעָם than is ἐν τῷ λαῷ. In the much more important matter of items 2–3, the ἄρχοντες τῶν προστατῶν of 2 Paralipomena reflects the construct שָׂרֵי, whereas the οἱ ἄρχοντες οἱ καθεσταμένοι does not. The practical implication of this is, as we have seen (p. 53), that v. h only has one group 'the officers who were appointed'; all the others have two groups, (1) the officers over (2) the deputies (foremen, chargehands). But the most crucial difference between v. h and the MT of 1 Kings is in its number: 3,600 is not the number of the *Israelite* officers, which is what the MT both of 1 Kings 9: 23 and 2 Chronicles 8: 10 is talking about, but the number which 2 Chronicles 2: 1 and 17 give for the *Gentile* foremen. Moreover the term v. h uses for them, ἐπιστάται, is exactly the same as the Greek of 1 Paralipomena 2: 1 (2) uses for the Gentile foremen. There is no mistaking, then, who these 3,600 ἐπιστάται are; but clearly their presence in v. h shows that somewhere along the line something has got muddled up.

56

Now, as we have already noticed, there is no counterpart in the main Greek text to v. h of Misc. 1 and to MT 9: 23, so that we cannot look to see if the main text is here as confused as the miscellany. On the other hand there is another passage in the main text which does speak of 3,600 ἐπιστάται, and it will be instructive to set it beside vv. d and h of Misc. 1.

Misc. 1	καὶ ἦν τῷ Σαλωμων	5: 29	καὶ ἦν τῷ Σαλωμων
v. d	ἑβδομήκοντα χιλιάδες		ἑβδομήκοντα χιλιάδες
	αἴροντες ἄρσιν		αἴροντες ἄρσιν
	καὶ ὀγδοήκοντα		καὶ ὀγδοήκοντα
	χιλιάδες		χιλιάδες
	λατόμων ἐν τῷ ὄρει.		λατόμων ἐν τῷ ὄρει.
Misc. 1	καὶ οὗτοι οἱ ἄρχοντες	5: 30	χωρὶς ἀρχόντων
v. h	οἱ καθεσταμένοι		τῶν καθεσταμένων
	ἐπὶ τὰ ἔργα τοῦ		ἐπὶ τῶν ἔργων τῶν
	Σαλωμων		Σαλωμων
	τρεῖς χιλιάδες καὶ		τρεῖς χιλιάδες καὶ
	ἑξακόσιοι ἐπιστάται		ἑξακόσιοι ἐπιστάται
	τοῦ λαοῦ		
	τῶν ποιούντων		οἱ ποιοῦντες
	τὰ ἔργα.		τὰ ἔργα.

It will be seen that whatever similarities they have, the miscellany and the main text disagree over one crucial point of interpretation: the miscellany makes only three distinct classes of men, the main text makes four. Both have 70,000 burden-bearers, both have 80,000 hewers; but then in Misc. 1 v. h οἱ ἄρχοντες οἱ καθεσταμένοι *are* the 3,600 ἐπιστάται, whereas in 5: 30 the 3,600 ἐπιστάται are said to be χωρὶς ἀρχόντων τῶν καθεσταμένων. And further to emphasise this difference, in 5: 30, if case usage can be relied on, the 3,600 ἐπιστάται are men who actually work themselves: they are working foremen. Of course, then, they are not the same as the officers: they are χωρὶς ἀρχόντων. But in Misc. 1 v. h the ἐπιστάται *are* the ἄρχοντες, and understandably, because they are officers, they do not work themselves: they are overseers of the people who do the work.

So then 5: 29–30 mentions all three classes of the Gentile levy exactly as we find them in Chronicles: the 70,000 burden bearers, the 80,000 hewers and the 3,600 working foremen; and in addition, as a fourth class, explicitly said to be separate from the other three, it mentions the ἀρχόντων τῶν καθεσταμένων ἐπὶ τῶν ἔργων τῶν Σαλωμων, who, of course, are meant to be none other than the (550 or 250) Israelite officers, spoken of in MT 1 Kings 9: 23 and 2 Chron. 8: 10. Now whether or not this interpretation can be justified by the underlying Hebrew – and this is a matter which we will look at in a moment – it means that the main Greek text is offering an interpretation that differs irreconcilably with the interpretation given in Misc. 1. Moreover, whatever authority the main text may or may not have from its Hebrew *vorlage*, its interpretation makes admirable sense, whereas the version offered by v. h of Misc. 1 confuses the Israelite officers with the 3,600 Gentile foremen, and is scarce worthy to be called an interpretation.

So far, then, our investigation has shown that v. h is not an approximation to its MT counterpart at 9: 23, and that it is in itself incorrect and confused. This at once suggests the probable reason why v. h stands in the miscellany at all: it was regarded as a rejected, or, at least, inferior, interpretation which could not be allowed to stand in the main text, for there it would clash with the interpretation given in 5: 30.

But it will be instructive to carry the investigation a little further and discover, if possible, how the confusion in v. h arose and whether the interpretation offered by the main text is true to the original Hebrew. The confusion, it would seem, was already present in the MT itself. At least the neat distinction which the main Greek text at 5: 30 draws between the Israelite officers (χωρὶς ἀρχόντων) and the Gentile foremen (3,600 ἐπιστάται), seems in the MT of 5: 30 either to have been blurred or never to have existed. This becomes the more apparent if we compare the MT of 5: 30 with the MT of 9: 23. The MT of 9: 23, as we saw above (p. 56) is talking of the

Israelite officers, yet its Hebrew bears a strong resemblance to the Hebrew of 5: 30, at the very point where according to the Greek it is supposed to be talking of the Gentile foremen. Here are the two MT verses side by side:

MT 1 Kings 5: 30	MT 1 Kings 9: 23
לְבַד	אֵלֶּה
מִשָּׂרֵי הַנִּצָּבִים	שָׂרֵי הַנִּצָּבִים
לִשְׁלֹמֹה	אֲשֶׁר עַל־הַמְּלָאכָה
אֲשֶׁר עַל־הַמְּלָאכָה	לִשְׁלֹמֹה
שְׁלֹשֶׁת אֲלָפִים	חֲמִשִּׁים
וּשְׁלֹשׁ מֵאוֹת	וַחֲמֵשׁ מֵאוֹת
הָרֹדִים בָּעָם	הָרֹדִים בָּעָם
הָעֹשִׂים בַּמְּלָאכָה׃	הָעֹשִׂים בַּמְּלָאכָה׃

The difference in the numbers, 3,300/550, is admittedly large. We will discuss it later. For the rest, apart from the introductory word and a minor difference in word order, the similarities are striking: both passages speak of שָׂרֵי הַנִּצָּבִים; both describe the same occupation הָרֹדִים בָּעָם – which incidentally is the expression which Chronicles uses to describe the occupation of the Israelite officers, whereas for the Gentile foremen it uses the term מְנַצְּחִים. But it is not only the similarity of phrase, but the similarity of sentence construction that is so telling. In 9: 23 the obvious way to construe the number and the participle הָרֹדִים is to take them as referring to שָׂרֵי. Admittedly שָׂרֵי is construct: 'officers of, or, over, the נִצָּבִים'; and so these שָׂרִים need not necessarily have belonged to the נִצָּבִים themselves, and, if it had not been for the intervening number, הָרֹדִים might conceivably have been intended to refer to הַנִּצָּבִים and not to שָׂרֵי, that is, the שָׂרֵי would then be officers over the-officials-who-ruled-among-the-people. But with the number intervening between the phrase שָׂרֵי הַנִּצָּבִים and the participle הָרֹדִים, and with the demonstrative אֵלֶּה picking out the שָׂרֵי for emphasis, the natural thing is to take both number and participle as referring to שָׂרֵי. And this, of course, is fine in 1 Kings 9: 23, for it gives a realistic number of Israelite chief officers, 550, and its description of their work, הָרֹדִים בָּעָם, is quite

unexceptionable. But the same logic applied to the syntax of
5: 30 will give us, not two classes of people, Israelite ἄρχοντες
and Gentile ἐπιστάται, but only one class, Israelite officers, שָׂרֵי
הַנִּצָּבִים הָרֹדִים בָּעָם... Admittedly this gives us a number for
the chief officers, 3,600, which is both unrealistic and discrepant
with the 550 of 9: 23. Moreover, it puts Israelite chief officers
where the context, the number, and analogy with Chronicles
would lead us to expect Gentile foremen. But can the Hebrew
legitimately be construed in any other way?

The Greek of 5: 30 attempts, as we have seen, to construe it
differently. To test the validity of its interpretation we should
now compare its translation with the Hebrew in detail.

1 Kings 5: 30	LXX 3 Reigns 5: 30 (BM 5: 16)
לְבַד מִשָּׂרֵי	χωρὶς ἀρχόντων
הַנִּצָּבִים	τῶν καθεσταμένων
לִשְׁלֹמֹה	ἐπὶ τῶν ἔργων
אֲשֶׁר עַל־הַמְּלָאכָה	τῶν Σαλωμων
שְׁלֹשֶׁת אֲלָפִים	τρεῖς χιλιάδες
וּשְׁלֹשׁ מֵאוֹת	καὶ ἑξακόσιοι
הָרֹדִים	ἐπιστάται
בָּעָם	
הָעֹשִׂים בַּמְּלָאכָה:	οἱ ποιοῦντες τὰ ἔργα.

There are two striking things about this translation. First, by
its case usage it makes quite clear that in its estimation neither
the numeral nor the participle הָרֹדִים is to be taken as referring
to שָׂרֵי. The לְבַד phrase is understood as running no further than
הַמְּלָאכָה, and accordingly in the Greek the χωρὶς phrase extends
only as far as Σαλωμων. The phrase is regarded as a parenthesis,
the contents of which are to be distinguished from what
follows. This then gives us two classes: the שָׂרֵי הַנִּצָּ" and the
3,600 (or 3,300) הָרֹדִים. Secondly, the translation construes the
final phrase הָעֹשִׂים בַּמְּלָאכָה as in apposition to הָרֹדִים and not to
בָּעָם.[6] This produces ἐπιστάται who are working foremen and so
all the more to be distinguished from the officers mentioned in
the parenthesis.

Now judged by the criterion of general sense and complete-
ness, the Greek interpretation is much to be preferred to the
apparent meaning of the MT. To start with, the Chronicler's
contention that from the large Gentile levy of 153,600 men,
3,600 Gentiles were appointed as working foremen, or chargehands, in control of their fellow Gentiles, and that over them
in turn were non-working Israelite officers – this contention is
reasonable enough. This state of affairs the Greek represents
fully:

1. 70,000 burden bearers
2. 80,000 hewers in the mountains
3. χωρὶς ἀρχόντων = Israelite officers
4. 3,600 foremen.

Moreover the order in which the Greek mentions the various
categories and the fact that it assigns no number to the Israelite
officers is very natural. It has mentioned the 70,000 burden
bearers and the 80,000 hewers, and is about to mention the
3,600 foremen, when it feels the need to distinguish these
Gentile foremen from the Israelite officers; so it slips in a brief
parenthetical phrase – 'apart from the chief officers that were
over the work' – without giving their number, since just the
bare mention of these officers is sufficient to distinguish them
from the 3,600 foremen.

The MT, on the other hand, is full of difficulties. In having
only three classes:

1. 70,000 burden bearers
2. 80,000 hewers
3. 3,300 (Israelite) chief officers,

it reduces the total Gentile levy to 150,000 and so disagrees with
the total given by the MT of 2 Chron. 2: 1 and 17; it brackets
Israelite chief officers somewhat indiscriminately with the
Gentile workmen; and its number of Israelite officers agrees not
with its own number (550) given in 9: 23, nor with the number
(250) given by 2 Chron. 8: 10, nor even with the number of
Gentile foremen (3,600) as given by 2 Chronicles and by the
Greek text of 1 Kings 5: 30 (and even by v. h of Misc. 1); its
number is a lone oddity.[7]

Nevertheless in spite of the advantages on the side of the Greek, it must be admitted that its interpretation does violence to the Hebrew of the MT. Of course it could easily be that the MT is at fault here, and that the Greek is founded on a Hebrew text that better represented the original. But given the MT's sequence ‏שְׁלֹשֶׁת אֲלָפִים וּשְׁלֹשׁ מֵאוֹת הָרֹדִים‎...‏לְבַד מִשָּׂרֵי הַנִּצָּבִים‎ the ‏ה‎ in front of ‏רֹדִים‎ makes it certain that ‏רֹדִים‎ is meant to refer to ‏מִשָּׂרֵי הַנִּצָּ"‎: apart from the chief officers, 3,300 '(the ones) who ruled...'. The Greek has to neglect this ‏ה‎ and its implication completely. Its translation χωρὶς ἀρχόντων...τρεῖς χιλιάδες καὶ ἑξακόσιοι ἐπιστάται would be fair only if the Hebrew read ‏שְׁלֹשֶׁת אֲלָפִים וּשְׁלֹשׁ מֵאוֹת רֹדִים‎, in the same way as 2 Chron. 2: 17 reads ‏שְׁלֹשֶׁת אֲלָפִים וְשֵׁשׁ מֵאוֹת מְנַצְּחִים‎ which, since ‏מְנַצְּחִים‎ is anarthrous, is fairly translated τρισχιλίους ἑξακοσίους ἐργοδιώκτας.

A lot, then, turns on the question whether the ‏ה‎ in ‏הָרֹדִים‎ of the MT is original or not. Happily we need not attempt to decide the issue, for the profit of this long discussion lies elsewhere. It has demonstrated that the present state of the main Greek text and of the miscellanies cannot be accounted for by the simple explanation that the Old Greek translation was made on the basis of a non-MT Hebrew manuscript, and then subsequently the Old Greek was supplemented by an editor who wished to make it conform to the MT. Behind the word for word duplication presented by v. d of Misc. 1 and the main Greek text at 5: 29; behind the fact that v. h of Misc. 1, so far from being duplicated word for word, has not even a counterpart in the main Greek text; behind the fact that the main Greek text at 5: 30 has an interpretation that disagrees with the facts as presented by v. h of Misc. 1, even though they are not strictly textual counterparts; and behind the fact that neither the interpretation offered by the main text nor that offered by v. h agrees with the MT of 5: 30; behind all this there seems to lie an awareness on the part of the Greek that some Hebrew texts were confusing, if not confused; followed by an attempt – whether based on a Hebrew *vorlage* or not, we cannot say, but certainly sharing the understanding of the facts as presented by 2 Chronicles – to lay down a satisfactory interpretation; which attempt involved stationing a less convincing interpretation in Misc. 1 at v. h, and the adoption in the main Greek text of the favoured interpretation to the exclusion of all else.

(2) THE CASE OF SOLOMON'S OFFERINGS

From Misc. 1

v. g καὶ Σαλωμων ἀνέφερεν τρὶς[8] ἐν τῷ ἐνιαυτῷ ὁλοκαυτώσεις καὶ εἰρηνικὰς ἐπὶ τὸ θυσιαστήριον ὃ ᾠκοδόμησεν τῷ κυρίῳ, καὶ ἐθυμία ἐνώπιον κυρίου. καὶ συνετέλεσεν τὸν οἶκον.

From the main Greek text

There is no counterpart anywhere in the main Greek text of 3 Reigns.

V. g, as we have already noticed (p. 11), is one of three verses in Misc. 1 which have their counterpart in MT at 9: 23–5. V. g's own counterpart is MT 9: 25, and the correspondence, though not complete, is nearly so. We naturally ask first why there is no counterpart in the main Greek text. It could be, of course, that v. g has no special reasons of its own[9] for standing in the miscellany rather than in the main Greek text, but that it was carried along thither in company with its companion verses f[βγ] and h when these two verses were dismissed to the miscellany because in the main text they would have clashed with the different interpretations which the main text adopted. But this possibility ought not to preclude an investigation of v. g in its own right.

The first step is to notice that the Hebrew of v. g's counterpart in the MT contains several difficulties. Most of them we may ignore since v. g follows the MT very closely in spite of these difficulties. But over one difficult phrase the Greek does depart somewhat from the MT, and this is instructive. The MT says of Solomon וְהַקְטִיר אִתּוֹ אֲשֶׁר לִפְנֵי יהוה. The RV translates 'burning incense therewith, upon the altar that was before the Lord', and it italicises the words 'upon the altar', indicating that, without justification from the MT, it has added these words because it judged that they were necessary to the sense. Actually the words אִתּוֹ אֲשֶׁר are very difficult, if not impossible, and to supply the words 'upon the altar' admits the difficulty without solving it. Many scholars[10] seem to accept Klostermann's emendation of אִתּוֹ אֲשֶׁר to אֶת־אִשָּׁיו *his fire-offerings*, and understand the verb הַקְטִיר in the sense, *make (sacrifices) smoke*, i.e. *offer sacrifices by fire*, and not in the sense *burn incense*. This gets over two difficulties: it makes sense of the difficult אתו אשר, and at the same time, instead of representing Solomon as burning incense, it represents him as offering burnt sacrifices (of animals and so forth) before the Lord. This would raise no difficulty in anyone's mind, since the phrase 'before the Lord' would then be understood to mean 'at the altar of burnt offering in the court of the temple', and non-priests could assist in the ceremony there; whereas to say '*Solomon burned incense before the Lord*' could only be understood as meaning that he officiated at the altar of incense in the Holy Place, which of course was forbidden to any but the priests. It was precisely for insisting on burning incense before the Lord that King Uzziah was smitten with leprosy (2 Chron. 26: 16–23). But the Greek of our v. g ignores both these difficulties. It has nothing for אתו אשר, and it takes הקטיר as *he burned incense*, καὶ ἐθυμία ἐνώπιον κυρίου.

Yet if v. g did not sense these points as difficulties, it would seem that the Chronicler did, as will be seen if we put the Kings passage and its counterpart in Chronicles side by side:

1 Kings 9: 25	2 Chron. 8: 12–16
And three times in a year did Solomon offer burnt offerings and peace offerings upon the altar which he built unto the Lord and burned incense (אתו אשר) before the Lord. So he	Then Solomon offered burnt offerings unto the Lord on the altar of the Lord, which he had built before the porch, even as the duty of every day required, offering according to the com-

finished the house.

mand of Moses, on the sab-
baths, and on the new moons,
and on the set feasts, three
times in the year, in the feast of
unleavened bread, and in the
feast of weeks, and in the feast
of tabernacles...So the house
of the Lord was perfected.

We notice at once that there is no mention in Chronicles of
Solomon burning incense before the Lord: the whole difficult
phrase והקטיר אתו אשר לפני יהיה is missing. On the other hand,
Chronicles has an extra phrase to make explicitly clear what
altar it was on which Solomon offered, and exactly where it
stood: the altar of the Lord, which he had built *before the porch*.
There is no danger here of anyone imagining that Solomon
approached the incense altar in the Holy Place!

Moreover, by its additions and detailed explanations
Chronicles avoids another difficulty in the Kings account. Kings
says simply that Solomon offered sacrifices three times a year.
These three times were doubtless, as Chronicles explains in
detail, on the occasions of the three great national festivals.
There is no need, of course, to interpret the statement in Kings
to mean that on only these three occasions did Solomon offer
any sacrifices; on the other hand, any pedant so inclined
might interpret it that way. No such danger in Chronicles!
The three times are still mentioned; but the phrase is explained,
and all the other occasions on which Solomon offered sacrifices
are recorded in detail.

If, then, the Chronicler felt these difficulties and went out of
his way to avoid them, it might well be that our v. g finds itself
in the miscellany rather than in the main Greek text, because
at some stage, someone felt it to be a difficult verse, and
removed it. And this would explain why no attempt was made
to put an alternative translation in the text. Short of re-writing
the verse completely, there was nothing one could do to avoid
the potential misunderstanding. The only other explanation

would be that the main Greek text was translated from a Hebrew *vorlage* that lacked this verse, and that someone later added v. g to the miscellany on the basis of the MT. But the fact that v. g ignores the אֹתוֹ אֲשֶׁר of the MT,[11] seems to go against this view.

(3) THE CASE OF SOLOMON'S WIFE

From Misc. 1

v. c καὶ ἔλαβεν τὴν θυγατέρα Φαραω καὶ εἰσήγαγεν αὐτὴν εἰς τὴν πόλιν Δαυιδ ἕως συντελέσαι αὐτὸν τὸν οἶκον αὐτοῦ καὶ[12] τὸν οἶκον Κυρίου ἐν πρώτοις καὶ τὸ τεῖχος Ιερουσαλημ κυκλόθεν· ἐν ἑπτὰ ἔτεσιν ἐποίησεν καὶ συνετέλεσεν.

v. f^{βγ} οὕτως θυγάτηρ Φαραω ἀνέβαινεν ἐκ τῆς πόλεως Δαυιδ εἰς τὸν οἶκον αὐτῆς, ὃν ᾠκοδόμησεν αὐτῇ.

From the main Greek text

5: 14a (BM 4: 31) καὶ ἔλαβεν Σαλωμων τὴν θυγατέρα Φαραω ἑαυτῷ εἰς γυναῖκα καὶ εἰσήγαγεν αὐτὴν εἰς τὴν πόλιν Δαυιδ ἕως συντελέσαι αὐτὸν τὸν οἶκον Κυρίου καὶ τὸν οἶκον ἑαυτοῦ καὶ τὸ τεῖχος Ιερουσαλημ.

9: 9a (BM 9: 9) τότε ἀνήγαγεν Σαλωμων τὴν θυγατέρα Φαραω ἐκ πόλεως Δαυιδ εἰς οἶκον αὐτοῦ ὃν ᾠκοδόμησεν αὐτῷ ἐν ταῖς ἡμέραις ἐκείναις.

Both verses in the miscellany have counterparts in the MT, and, as is evident, both verses have counterparts in the main Greek text. But neither of the counterparts in the main Greek text occupies the same position as its counterpart in the MT. The counterpart of Misc. 1 v. c in the MT is at 3: 1 (not 5: 14a), and of v. f^{βγ} at 9: 24 (not 9: 9a).

Now vv. c and f^{βγ} quite obviously form a pair as do 5: 14a and 9: 9a. Each pair is dealing with the two parts of the one story: the putting of Pharaoh's daughter into the city of David and the bringing of her out again. All four verses must therefore be discussed together. Some of the verses we have already (pp. 18–23) discussed in connection with the position of v. f in Misc. 1 and with the midrashic interpretation that this verse has been made to serve. Before we are finished, we shall find these verses involve us in midrash again; but for the moment our first aim is to enquire where the material came from before it was turned to midrashic use. It will be best, therefore, to start with the second member of each pair because with them it is easy to see that differing Hebrew texts lie behind some, at least, of their peculiarities.

MT 1 Kings 9: 24	LXX Misc. 1 f^βγ	LXX 3 Reigns 9: 9a	MT 2 Chron. 8: 11	LXX 2 Paralip. 8: 11
אַךְ	οὕτως	τότε	וְאֶת־	καὶ τὴν
בַּת־	θυγάτηρ	ἀνήγαγεν	בַּת־פַּר"	θυγατέρα Φ.
פַּרְעֹה	Φαραω	Σαλωμων	הֶעֱלָה	Σαλωμων
עָלְתָה	ἀνέβαινεν	τὴν θυγατέρα Φ.	שְׁלֹמֹה	ἀνήγαγεν
מֵעִיר	ἐκ τῆς πόλεως	ἐκ πόλεως	מֵעִיר	ἐκ πόλεως
דָּוִד	Δαυιδ	Δαυιδ	דָּוִד	Δαυιδ
אֶל־	εἰς τὸν	εἰς		εἰς τὸν
בֵּיתָהּ	οἶκον αὐτῆς	οἶκον αὐτοῦ	לַבַּיִת	οἶκον
אֲשֶׁר	ὃν	ὃν	אֲשֶׁר	ὃν
בָּנָה־	ᾠκοδόμησεν	ᾠκοδόμησεν	בָּנָה־	ᾠκοδόμησεν
לָהּ	αὐτῇ.	αὐτῷ	לָהּ	αὐτῇ
אָז	τότε	ἐν		
בָּנָה	ᾠκοδόμησεν	ταῖς		
אֶת־	τὴν	ἡμέραις		
הַמִּלּוֹא׃	ἄκραν	ἐκείναις.		

The Hebrew texts cited above differ in two main respects: the MT of Kings says that 'Pharaoh's daughter came up', the MT of Chronicles that 'Solomon brought up Pharaoh's daughter'; in the MT of Kings there is appended a mention of the building of τὴν ἄκραν, but not so in Chronicles. And in both these respects Misc. 1 follows the MT of Kings, while the main Greek text of 3 Reigns agrees with the MT of Chronicles.

On the other hand the main Greek text does not agree completely with the MT of Chronicles: its τότε at the beginning and its ἐν ταῖς ἡμέραις ἐκείναις at the end are both peculiar to itself. Moreover they are both time-indicators whose meaning will be determined by the position of their verse in the text. And since, as we have seen, the positioning of this verse at 9: 9a is also peculiar to the main Greek text of Reigns, we have in this peculiar interest in the timing of the operation a very prominent feature of the main Greek text which is not based on the MT either of Kings or of Chronicles.

We naturally look next to see what meaning the verse's peculiar position will give to its time-indicators. Investigation shows that the positioning is very deliberate and connected with another, earlier peculiarity in the main text's order, the positioning of 5: 14a, the counterpart of Misc. 1 v. c. The sequence is:

5: 14a   Solomon puts Pharaoh's daughter in David's city until completion of the Lord's house, his own house, and the wall of Jerusalem.

5: 14b   Pharaoh's parting gift to his daughter.

5: 15–9: 9   Building of Lord's house and Solomon's palaces. Dedication of house. When all the building is finished, God appears to Solomon.

9: 9a   Solomon brings up Pharaoh's daughter out of David's city into his house.

One can see immediately the rationale of this arrangement. 5: 14a says that Solomon put Pharaoh's daughter in David's city *until* certain building should be complete. The very moment it is complete, 9: 9a is there to say that Solomon brought her up from David's city. One has only to realise, moreover, that the counterparts in the MT of 5: 14a and b stand at 3: 1b and 9: 16 respectively, to see how deliberate, and peculiar to itself, the Greek's order is, and how interested it is in the exact timings of the comings and goings of Pharaoh's daughter. (See further, p. 130 n. 22a.)

Furthermore we can now see that one of the main text's agreements with the MT of Chronicles, namely ἀνήγαγεν = הֶעֱלָה rather than ἀνέβαινεν = עָלְתָה, is clearly calculated to make 9: 9a play its part effectively in this strict timetable scheme. After 5: 14a καὶ ἔλαβεν Σαλωμων τὴν θυγατέρα Φαραω...καὶ εἰσήγαγεν αὐτὴν εἰς τὴν πόλιν Δαυιδ ἕως... the phrase τότε ἀνήγαγεν Σαλωμων τὴν θυγατέρα Φαραω... is more directly apposite than οὕτως θυγάτηρ Φαραω ἀνέβαινεν.

There is, moreover, a third feature in which the main text at 9: 9a goes its own way compared with all other texts; but it will be convenient to delay examination of that until we consider the first members of each pair. To complete our study of the second member of each pair, we have now to look at v. f^{βγ} of Misc. 1. This need not detain us long. It is an exact reproduction of the MT, except for one very significant difference: the first word has apparently been changed to make the verse fit into the miscellany's exegesis. We have already discussed this at length (p. 20); all we need add here is, that although v. f^{βγ} is far nearer to the MT than the main text is, yet had its motive been to 'correct' the main text on the basis of the MT, it would surely have followed the MT in its first word as in all the rest.

Now we may take the first members of each pair.

MT 3: 1	Misc. 1 v. c	Main text 5: 14a
וַיִּתְחַתֵּן שְׁלֹמֹה		
אֶת־פַּרְעֹה		
מֶלֶךְ מִצְרָיִם		
וַיִּקַּח	καὶ ἔλαβεν	καὶ ἔλαβεν
		Σαλωμων
אֶת־בַּת־	τὴν θυγατέρα	τὴν θυγατέρα
פַּרְעֹה	Φαραω	Φαραω
		ἑαυτῷ
		εἰς γυναῖκα
וַיְבִיאֶהָ	καὶ εἰσήγαγεν αὐτὴν	καὶ εἰσήγαγεν αὐτὴν
אֶל־עִיר	εἰς τὴν πόλιν	εἰς τὴν πόλιν
דָּיִד	Δαυιδ	Δαυιδ
עַד כַּלֹּתוֹ לִבְנוֹת	ἕως συντελέσαι αὐτὸν	ἕως συντελέσαι αὐτὸν
אֶת־בֵּיתוֹ	[τὸν οἶκον αὐτοῦ	τὸν οἶκον Κυρίου

69

MT 3: 1	Misc. 1 v. c	Main text 5: 14a
וְאֶת בֵּית יהוה	καὶ]¹³ τὸν οἶκον	καὶ τὸν οἶκον
	Κυρίου	ἑαυτοῦ
	ἐν πρώτοις	
וְאֶת־חוֹמַת	καὶ τὸ τεῖχος	καὶ τὸ τεῖχος
יְרוּשָׁלֵם	Ιερουσαλημ	Ιερουσαλημ
סָבִיב	κυκλόθεν	

MT 6: 38ᵇ		6: 38ᵇ
וַיִּבְנֵהוּ	ἐν ἑπτὰ ἔτεσιν	—
שֶׁבַע שָׁנִים	ἐποίησεν	—
	καὶ συνετέλεσεν.	—

The first thing to notice is that neither the main text nor the miscellany follows the MT exactly. Indeed, in the most crucial phrase of all they disagree with it. The MT's introductory clause says '*And Solomon made affinity with Pharaoh king of Egypt*', which puts beyond doubt that Solomon married Pharaoh's daughter. But without the introductory clause, the next clause '*and he took the daughter of Pharaoh*' could be ambiguous: it need not necessarily imply that he took her to wife, but simply that he took her, married or unmarried, about to be married or never to be. It would, of course, seem most unreasonable to suggest that any Biblical text could raise a doubt as to whether Solomon actually married Pharaoh's daughter. But in later times, we know, the rabbis did disagree on this point. The disagreement arose over the question whether marriages between certain classes of Israelites and a nethinah or an idolatress were valid. Raba stated:[14]

...while they are still idolators their marriages are invalid; only when they are converted are their marriages valid. R. Joseph raised an objection: *And Solomon became allied to Pharaoh King of Egypt by marriage, and took Pharaoh's daughter.* – He caused her to be converted. But, surely, no proselytes were accepted either in the days of David or in the days of Solomon...R. Papa replied: Are we to take our directions from Solomon! Solomon did not marry at all, for it is written, *Of the nations concerning which the Lord said... Ye shall not go among them...Solomon did cleave unto them in love.*[15] The expression, *And he became allied...in marriage*, however, presents a difficulty! – On account of his excessive love for her, Scripture regards him as if he had become allied by marriage to her.

Now whatever we think about the Talmud's exegesis here, it is noticeable that the phrase which some rabbis found difficult – *And Solomon became allied...in marriage* – is the very one which has no direct counterpart in either the main text or the miscellany. The main text, however, compensates for this omission by adding after the verb ἔλαβεν (seemingly on its own authority) the phrase ἑαυτῷ εἰς γυναῖκα: the main text, at least, commits itself to the view that Solomon actually married Pharaoh's daughter. Not so the miscellany: it has no compensatory phrase,[16] and this difference between the miscellany and the main text is presumably deliberate and is one of the reasons why the verse originally came to stand in the miscellany at all. If so, it would seem that a difference in exegesis lies behind the existence of these variants.

The next difference of major importance between the miscellany and both the main text and the MT, is that Misc. 1 adds at the end of the verse the sentence: ἐν ἑπτὰ ἔτεσιν ἐποίησεν καὶ συνετέλεσεν. We have already seen (p. 11) where Misc. 1 is likely to have obtained this material, and that its presence in this position in the miscellany is the work of the editor. Now we are to see that by introducing this clause here the editor contradicts the main text. Both he and the main text are keenly interested in Pharaoh's daughter being placed temporarily in David's city, the length of her stay there, and the exact timing of her departure; but the miscellany will have it that he finished in seven years. It does not say explicitly in v. c^{β} exactly what he finished; so one can only conclude that the καὶ συνετέλεσεν is picking up the ἕως συντελέσαι of the earlier part of the verse. This would mean that what he finished in seven years was all[17] the building necessary before he could bring Pharaoh's daughter up out of the city of David. The main text, however, disagrees with this, and maintains that it was twenty years before all the necessary building was finished. At 8:1, in a clause which here has no counterpart in the MT, it says καὶ ἐγένετο ὡς συνετέλεσεν Σαλωμων τοῦ οἰκοδομῆσαι τὸν οἶκον Κυρίου καὶ τὸν οἶκον ἑαυτοῦ μετὰ εἴκοσι ἔτη (he assembled all Israel, dedicated the temple; then God appeared to him in a vision, and then he brought up Pharaoh's daughter). So once more we have an exegetical reason behind the difference between the miscellany and the main text.

At this juncture we may recur to the third difference between the main Greek text at 9: 9a and all the other texts (see p. 67). If we look back to p. 67, we shall see that whereas all the other texts, both Greek and Hebrew, phrase themselves thus '*her* (or, the) house which Solomon built for *her*', the main Greek text has '*his* house which he built for *himself*'. One can, of course, only speculate on the possible significance of this difference. But it is the fact that some of the later rabbis who held that Solomon actually married Pharaoh's daughter taught that he married her only upon the completion of the temple, on the night, in fact, before the dedication of the temple, seven years after he began to build the temple. See for instance Midrash Rabbah,[18] *Numbers* x, 4: 'On the selfsame night that Solomon completed the work of the Holy Temple he married Bathiah, the daughter of Pharaoh...'; and Midrash Rabbah,[19] *Leviticus* xii, 5: 'R. Judah said: All the seven years during which Solomon was building the Temple he did not drink wine. After he had built it and taken Bithiah, the daughter of Pharaoh, to wife, he drank wine that night...' That Solomon should wait seven years before actually marrying Pharaoh's daughter is, of course, a most unlikely story; but it is apparently derived from the verse, 1 Kings 3: 1, 'Solomon made affinity with Pharaoh king of Egypt, and took Pharaoh's daughter and brought her into the city of David until he had made an end of building...the house of the Lord...' The verse is understood to mean that though he made affinity with Pharaoh and took his daughter, he did not there and then marry her, but put her in David's city, and only married her after the temple was built. On this interpretation 'bringing up Pharaoh's daughter out of the city of David' would then be the equivalent of 'actually marrying her'. Now as we have already seen (p. 67), the main Greek text at 9: 9a prefers the expression 'Solomon brought up the daughter of Pharaoh' to the expression 'The daughter of Pharaoh came up'. Clearly the former expression is more suited if it is intended to carry the meaning 'he actually married her'. But, in addition, it is easily seen that the phrasing peculiar to the main Greek text, 'into *his* house which he had built for *himself*' would again be much more suitable for conveying the nuance 'he actually married her', than the phrasing of all the other texts 'into *her* house which he had built for *her*'. Perhaps, then, the main Greek text is an early instance of the interpretation which held that Solomon did not actually marry Pharaoh's daughter when he took her and put her in David's city, but only at, or after, the completion and dedication of the temple. It would, of course, involve the main text, because of its peculiar and emphatic timetable (8: 1), in the absurdity that it was twenty years from the time he took her to the time he married her; but absurdity is no embarrassment to a midrashic exegete.

What we seem to have then in the main Greek text is one feature based on a Hebrew text different from the MT of 1 Kings (but agreeing with the MT of Chronicles), and, for the rest, peculiarities which, in the limited state of our knowledge, are not traceable beyond the main Greek text itself. The resultant whole, however, is fitted into a scheme of interpretation that is no less midrashic than the alternative scheme, dealing with the same topic, in Misc. 1. And the fact that two alternative schemes of interpretation are offered seems to reflect an early debate on this topic, which in later times was so much discussed, Solomon's marriage to Pharaoh's daughter.

(4) THE CASE OF SOLOMON'S LUNCHEON

From Misc. 2

v. e καὶ τοῦτο τὸ ἄριστον τῷ Σαλωμων (ἐν ἡμέρᾳ μιᾷ)[20]...καὶ ἑκατὸν πρόβατα ἐκτὸς ἐλάφων καὶ δορκάδων καὶ ὀρνίθων ἐκλεκτῶν νομάδων.

From the main Greek text

5: 2–3 (BM 4: 22–3) καὶ ταῦτα τὰ δέοντα τῷ Σαλωμων ἐν ἡμέρᾳ μιᾷ...καὶ ἑκατὸν πρόβατα ἐκτὸς ἐλάφων καὶ δορκάδων καὶ ὀρνίθων ἐκλεκτῶν σιτευτά.

The two long lists of Solomon's provisions are remarkable for their almost word for word agreement. The many details in which they agree have therefore been omitted here; we need only consider the disagreements. One of these comes at the end. In the MT the list ends: וַיַחְמוּר וּבַרְבֻּרִים אֲבוּסִים, which the NEB translates as 'roebucks and fattened fowl'. But both the miscellany and the main text have ὀρνίθων as the antepenultimate item, which, if it stands for יַחְמוּר, is wrong. Both again omit the waw before וּבַרְבֻּרִים, translate בַּרְבֻּרִים itself as ἐκλεκτῶν and refer it to ὀρνίθων. This mistake then leaves both of them with the single word אֲבוּסִים, which, since it has no copula, is awkward and can only be treated as an adjective. But here each translation goes its own way. The miscellany just tags on νομάδων, which as an adjective describing birds is not the happiest. The main text has a radically different solution: it uses the adjective σιτευτά and refers it not to ὀρνίθων but to the earlier πρόβατα. 'Fattened sheep' makes perhaps better sense than 'pastured birds'; but the long gap between the noun and adjective – 100 sheep (besides stags, and gazelles, and choice birds) fattened – is very awkward. But while neither could be called a satisfactory translation, perhaps πρόβατα...σιτευτά is slightly the better, and this may account for its standing in the main text.

At the beginning of the list however there is a much more important difference, and this time there is no doubt that the main text's translation makes much better sense than that of the miscellany. Neither offers a literal translation of לֶחֶם, for obviously לֶחֶם does not here mean 'bread' but 'provisions'. Of this τὰ δέοντα, 'necessities', is a reasonable enough translation. But ἄριστον is absurd: rich as Solomon was, the many items of flour, meal, calves, oxen, sheep, stags, gazelles and fowl here described, served clearly for more than Solomon's lunch. The translation ἄριστον is either a mistake, which has been rejected in preference for the better rendering of the main text, or it could be a deliberate haggadic exaggeration; and in its own context in the miscellany we get a hint that the latter explanation is the correct one.

In the MT the context of the verse is as follows:

5: 2–3　Solomon's daily provisions.

4　For Solomon was ruling (over a large area)...and he had peace...

5　And Judah and Israel dwelt safely, every man under his vine and under his fig tree, from Dan even to Beersheba, all the days of Solomon.

Now this last verse, 5: 5, is very similar to an earlier verse, 4: 20, 'Judah and Israel were many, as the sand which is by the sea in multitude, eating and drinking and making merry.' The difference is that 5: 5 is thinking of the nation's *security* from foreign attack rather than its prosperity as a result of foreign tribute; 5: 5, therefore, does not mention the nation's 'eating and drinking'. Turning to Misc. 2, we find it has an exact counterpart of MT 4: 20 standing at v. a$^\beta$. It has also a counterpart of MT 5: 5, standing in exactly the same position as the MT's verse,[31] but with one tell-tale difference:

v. e　καὶ τοῦτο τὸ ἄριστον τῷ Σαλωμων...

f, g$^\alpha$　ὅτι ἦν ἄρχων...καὶ ἦν αὐτῷ εἰρήνη...

g$^\beta$　καὶ κατῴκει Ιουδα καὶ Ισραηλ πεποιθότες, ἕκαστος ὑπὸ τὴν ἄμπελον αὐτοῦ καὶ ὑπὸ τὴν συκῆν αὐτοῦ, <u>ἐσθίοντες καὶ πίνοντες</u> ἀπὸ Δαν καὶ ἕως Βηρσαβεε πάσας τὰς ἡμέρας Σαλωμων.

Of course, ἐσθίοντες καὶ πίνοντες may have been added under the influence of ἐσθίοντες καὶ πίνοντες καὶ χαίροντες in the nearby v. a$^\beta$, and its presence in v. g$^\beta$ may be, therefore, nothing more than an accident. But we have hitherto found that many of the miscellany's peculiarities are deliberate and midrashic; it may be that this one is too, for vv. e and g$^\beta$, as they now stand, have three features in common with the discussion of Solomon's provisions that we find in the Babylonian Talmud,[22] *Baba Mezia*, 86b:

Shall we say that the meals of Abraham, the Patriarch, were superior to those of Solomon; but is it not written, And Solomon's provisions for one day were thirty measures of fine flour, and three score measures of meal. Ten fat oxen, and twenty oxen out of the pastures, and an hundred sheep, besides harts, and roebucks, and fallowdeer, and fatted fowl: whereon Gorion b. Astion said in Rab's name: These were but for the cook's dough;[23] and R. Isaac said: These (animals) were but for the (mincemeat) puddings. Moreover, said R. Isaac, Solomon had a thousand wives, and each prepared this quantity in her own house. Why? Each reasoned, 'He may dine in my house to-day'. Whereas of Abraham it is said, *And Abraham ran unto the herd and fetched a calf tender and good*: whereon Rab observed: '*A calf*', means one; '*tender*' – two; and '*good*' – three! – There the three calves were for three men, whereas here (the provisions enumerated) were for all Israel and Judah, as it is written, *Judah and Israel were many, as the sand which is by the sea in multitude*.

What is meant by '*fatted fowl*'? – Rab said: (Fowls) fed against their will. Samuel said: (Fowls) naturally fat. R. Johanan said: Oxen which had never toiled were brought from the pastures, and likewise fowls (that had never toiled) from their dungheaps.

The first point in common between this discussion and Misc. 2 is the deliberate exaggeration. Solomon's vast provisions are said to be only 'for the cook's dough' or 'for the mincemeat puddings'. So with the ἄριστον of Misc. 2: it is not a literal translation of לֶחֶם any more than τὰ δέοντα is; but it is an exaggeration which makes out that the entire provisions for one day actually sufficed for one meal only, his lunch. Secondly, the Talmud maintains that the provisions enumerated were not for Solomon only but for the whole of Judah and Israel.[24] Similarly the introduction of ἐσθίοντες καὶ πίνοντες in v. g[β] (see p. 75) might well be a deliberate insertion to 'explain' that the large amount of provisions for Solomon's luncheon fed Judah and Israel as well. Thirdly the discussion of the meaning of '*fatted fowl*' covers the words which we examined above (p. 74) and shows that later scholars found it difficult to decide their meaning, just as the Greek translations did.

But whatever the truth is about these suggestions, two things can be said with certainty: the difference between Misc. 2 and the main text, at least over the translation ἄριστον/τὰ δέοντα does not imply difference of Hebrew *vorlage*, nor is the translation in Misc. 2 an approximation to the MT.

(6) THE CASE OF SOLOMON'S MINISTERS[25]

From Misc. 2

v. h καὶ οὗτοι οἱ ἄρχοντες τοῦ Σαλωμων· Αζαριου υἱὸς
Σαδωκ τοῦ ἱερέως καὶ Ορνιου υἱὸς Ναθαν ἄρχων τῶν ἐφεστηκό-
των καὶ Εδραμ ἐπὶ τὸν οἶκον αὐτοῦ καὶ Σουβα γραμματεὺς καὶ
Βασα υἱὸς Αχιθαλαμ ἀναμιμνήσκων καὶ Αβι υἱὸς Ιωαβ ἀρχι-
στράτηγος καὶ Αχιρε υἱὸς Εδραϊ ἐπὶ τὰς ἄρσεις καὶ Βαναια υἱὸς
Ιωδαε ἐπὶ τῆς αὐλαρχίας καὶ ἐπὶ τοῦ πλινθείου καὶ Ζαχουρ υἱὸς
Ναθαν ὁ σύμβουλος.

From the main Greek text

4: 1–6 καὶ οὗτοι οἱ ἄρχοντες, οἱ ἦσαν αὐτοῦ· Αζαριου υἱὸς
Σαδωκ καὶ Ελιαρεφ καὶ Αχια γραμματεῖς καὶ Ιωσαφατ υἱὸς
Αχιλιδ ὑπομιμνήσκων καὶ Σαδουχ καὶ Αβιαθαρ ἱερεῖς καὶ Ορνια
υἱὸς Ναθαν ἐπὶ τῶν καθεσταμένων καὶ Ζαβουθ υἱὸς Ναθαν
ἑταῖρος τοῦ βασιλέως καὶ Αχιηλ οἰκονόμος καὶ Ελιαβ υἱὸς Σαφ
ἐπὶ τῆς στρατιᾶς[26] καὶ Αδωνιραμ υἱὸς Εφρα ἐπὶ τῶν φόρων.

The MT's counterpart of these two passages is found at 4: 2–6.
Now long lists of names fall an easy prey to scribal error and
also to adaptation on the basis of similar lists elsewhere,[27] and it
would be tedious to discuss in detail all the many variants and
the emendations proposed by various scholars.[28] The passages
cited above are therefore given in the text as restored by Rahlfs
(with one exception: see n. 26), which is sufficiently exact for the
moment.

It is clear from a glance that the miscellany and the main
Greek text differ irreconcilably in many particulars. Both of
them in turn also differ from the MT in many respects, so that
one can say at once that neither is Misc. 2 an attempt to supplement or correct the main Greek text on the basis of the MT,
nor is the main Greek text closely conformed to the MT, even
though in many points it is nearer to the MT than is Misc. 2.
Moreover the differences between the MT, the main Greek text
and Misc. 2 are not merely matters of the spelling of proper

names: major points of substance are also involved. To see what those differences are it will be simplest if we take the MT phrase by phrase and compare it with the two Greek lists; though we do not, of course, imply by this procedure that the MT necessarily represents the original Hebrew better than the Greek lists do.

Item 1

MT   וְאֵלֶּה הַשָּׂרִים אֲשֶׁר־לוֹ

Misc. 2   οὗτοι οἱ ἄρχοντες τοῦ Σαλωμων

MGT[29] οὗτοι οἱ ἄρχοντες οἱ ἦσαν αὐτοῦ

The οἱ ἦσαν αὐτοῦ of the MGT is nearer[30] the אֲשֶׁר־לוֹ of the MT than is τοῦ Σαλωμων of Misc. 2.

Item 2

MT   עֲזַרְיָהוּ בֶן־צָדוֹק הַכֹּהֵן

Misc. 2   Αзαριου υἱὸς Σαδωκ τοῦ ἱερέως

MGT   Αзαριου υἱὸς Σαδωκ

We may here neglect the variants in the spelling of Αзαριου.[31] The main point of interest is what the Greek translations do with the word הַכֹּהֵן, 'the priest'. The miscellany puts it in the genitive case, τοῦ ἱερέως, so making it refer to Zadok. But this cannot represent the original Hebrew, for the sentence thus simply tells us that Azariu was son of Zadok the priest, and does not say what his own office was. Moreover, apart from this indirect reference to the office of priest, this list is now left without any direct mention of the priest's office, and this is obviously wrong. Perhaps the translator was misled by the article in front of כֹּהֵן, and mistakenly took the noun as being in apposition to צָדוֹק; though a little lower down a similarly patterned phrase in the MT, יְהוֹשָׁפָט בֶּן־אֲחִילוּד הַמַּזְכִּיר, has as its counterpart in the miscellany Βασα υἱὸς Αχιθαλαμ ἀναμιμνήσκων (not τοῦ ἀναμιμνήσκοντος). Or it could be that the translator was so used to the phrase 'Zadok the priest', that he automatically and without thinking made 'the priest' agree with 'Zadok'. But there seems to be more to it than that; for while lower in the list the MT (4: 4) has 'And Zadok and Abiathar were priests', the miscellany lacks this phrase completely, and this is hardly an accidental omission. Similarly, while the MT says (4: 5) 'And Zabud, the son of Nathan, was Priest, King's Friend', the miscellany simply says Ζαχουρ υἱὸς Ναθαν ὁ σύμβουλος, i.e. it leaves out the title 'Priest'. Again this is hardly accidental. It is more likely (1) that since the MT and the main Greek text at 2: 27 say 'So Solomon thrust out Abiathar from being priest unto the Lord', the miscellany has withheld all reference to Abiathar's being priest; (2) that it has withheld the title 'Priest' from Zachur, because it did not understand this title being used of any except members of the religious Levitical priesthood;[32] (3) that having thus disposed of all 'dubious' references to priests, it has contented itself with its indirect reference to Zadok the priest at the beginning, although its translation there is mistaken.

The main Greek text agrees, apparently, with the miscellany over the main point that Αζαριου was not priest; but instead of reading 'priest' in apposition to 'Zadok', it omits the word 'priest' altogether, and is thus further from the MT in this particular than Misc. 2 is; moreover it brackets Αζαριου with the following group and so turns him into a scribe, thus: Αζαριου υἱὸς Σαδωκ καὶ Ελιαρεφ καὶ Αχια υἱὸς Σαβα γραμματεῖς.

Similarly, the main Greek text (4: 5) agrees in one point with the miscellany later on over the son of Nathan: while it calls him Ζαβουθ, whereas Misc. 2 calls him Ζαχουρ, and styles him ἑταῖρος τοῦ βασιλέως while Misc. 2 calls him ὁ σύμβουλος, it agrees with Misc. 2 against the MT in *not* calling him 'priest'.

Finally, the main text agrees with Misc. 2 that Zadok was the priest; but unlike the miscellany it has a direct statement to that effect, and it includes Abiathar in the priesthood with him: (4: 4) καὶ Σαδουχ καὶ Αβιαθαρ ἱερεῖς. In this it is closer to the MT than Misc. 2 is.

It is clear, then, that these variations between the MT, the main Greek text and Misc. 2 are not accidental: they stem from a disagreement over who was priest under Solomon, and from a difference of opinion on whether any official other than a minister in the temple could be called a priest.

Item 3

MT   אֱלִיחֹרֶף וַאֲחִיָּה בְּנֵי שִׁישָׁא סֹפְרִים[33]

Misc. 2   καὶ Σουβα γραμματεύς

MGT   καὶ Ελιαρεφ καὶ Αχια υἱὸς Σαβα γραμματεῖς

It is obvious that in content the main Greek text is fairly close to the MT, while Misc. 2 is much farther from it. Moreover, while in the MT the two scribes are the second item in the list and in the main Greek text they are the first item (because Αζαριου has been bracketed with them as a scribe), in Misc. 2 there is but one scribe and he stands fourth in the list; so that in this respect too the main Greek text is nearer the MT than Misc. 2 is.

When it comes to the name Σαβα–Σουβα, the differences in the manuscripts both of the main Greek text and of Misc. 2 make it difficult to be certain of the original Greek form;[34] but the main variants quite clearly go back to different Hebrew readings. In the main Greek text Σαβα goes back to שְׁוָא, the Ķrê of 2 Sam. 20: 25. Σεισα of the majority represents שִׁישָׁא, the reading of MT 1 Kings 4: 3, and is doubtless Origenic. *Susa*, read by La. in the main text, and by the Lucianics and La. in Misc. 2, looks like the שׁושׁא of 1 Chron. 18: 16 read as שׁוּשָׁא instead of שַׁוְשָׁא. Indeed, the majority Greek text of 1 Chron. 18: 16 reads Σουσα. But neither Σαβα, which is probably the original reading in the main text, nor Σουβα, the majority reading in Misc. 2, agrees with the MT of 1 Kings 4: 3.

Item 4

MT   יְהוֹשָׁפָט בֶּן־אֲחִילוּד הַמַּזְכִּיר

Misc. 2   καὶ Βασα υἱὸς Αχιθαλαμ ἀναμιμνῄσκων

MGT   καὶ Ιωσαφατ υἱὸς Αχιλιδ ὑπομιμνῄσκων

Once again the main Greek text is much nearer the MT than Misc. 2 is, though it is interesting to note that for the patronymic, the Lucianic MSS read Αχιθαλαμ (vel sim.), so having here in the main text the reading which the majority have in Misc. 2 (with which they also agree *in loco*). On the other hand it is only the Lucianics with Ba₂ that read ὑπομιμνήσκων in the main text, as against the ἀναμιμνήσκων of the majority in the main text and of the complete evidence (themselves included) for Misc. 2. Again in Misc. 2 it is the Lucianics that dispute the majority text in reading Βαρακ instead of Βασα;[35] so that in the end the Lucianic text agrees fully neither with the main Greek text nor with Misc. 2. Interesting variations in the name and office of this same officer occur elsewhere: in 2 Sam. 20: 24, for the majority text καὶ Ιωσαφατ υἱὸς Αχιλουθ ἀναμιμνήσκων, the Lucianics have Σαφαν υἱὸς Αχιθαλαα ὑπομιμνήσκων, while in 1 Chron. 18: 15, which has Ιωσαφατ υἱὸς Αχιλουδ ὑπομνηματογράφος, the minuscule e₂ (normally a member of the Lucianic group) substitutes for ὑπομνηματογράφος, the term ἀναμιμνήσκων (and not ὑπομιμνήσκων as one might expect). Finally, in 4 Reigns 18: 18, 37 ὁ ἀναμιμνήσκων is the undisputed term for the office.

In view of this one might perhaps be tempted to argue that in the Books of Reigns ὑπομιμνήσκων represents an early translation, and ἀναμιμνήσκων a later translation or revision.[36] On this argument the original text would be represented in 2 Reigns 20: 24 by the Lucianics alone, and in 3 Reigns 4: 3 by the Lucianics plus Ba₂ only; and this would fit in well with Barthélemy's theory that in these parts of the Books of Reigns the Lucianics tend to present an older text than the other manuscripts.[37] But this would in fact lead to a contradictious result. It would mean that Misc. 2, which uses ἀναμιμνήσκων, is a later translation than the Ba₂–Lucianic version of the main Greek text, which uses ὑπομιμνήσκων; and yet in all other details in this item Misc. 2 is the farthest of any away from the MT, when, if it were a later translation, one would expect it to be the nearest to the MT. We must therefore content ourselves with the general statement that while on the whole the main-text traditions are nearer to the MT than the Misc. 2 traditions are, all traditions in this item have suffered more or less confusion[38] arising perhaps in part from differences in the underlying Hebrew texts, and aggravated by contamination from parallel passages, by revisory activity in the Greek mss, and by scribal error.

Item 5

MT   וּבְנָיָהוּ בֶן־יְהוֹיָדָע עַל־הַצָּבָא

Misc. 2   καὶ Αβι υἱὸς Ιωαβ ἀρχιστράτηγος

The significant variants are:

αβι] αβια i Eth.: ελιαβ Z (uid.) boc₂e₂ dgp La.

ιωαβ] ιωαμ h* (uid.): ιωαδ b

ἀρχιστράτηγος] αρχιστρατηγου i

Cf. the later item: καὶ Βαναια(ς) υἱὸς Ιωδαε (ιωαδ Zoc₂e₂ dp) ἐπὶ τῆς αὐλαρχίας καὶ ἐπὶ τοῦ πλινθείου.

MGT   4: 4

Bva₂ Eth.:   NIL

MNZ boc₂e₂ ghiny La.: Βαναιας (βανεας be) υἱὸς Ιωδαε (ιωδας M: ιωαδ Z (uid.) boc₂e₂: ιωιαδαε La.) ἐπὶ τῆς δυναμέως (δυναμεως periit in Z: dux virtutis La.).

A rell. Syr. (sub ※ θ′): Βαναιας υἱὸς Ιωδαε (om. υιος ιωδαε d: υιος ιωιαδαε A) ἐπὶ τῆς στρατιᾶς (vel στρατείας).[39]

  4: 6

BAMN plures Eth. Syr.: Ελιαβ υἱὸς Σαφ (σαφα Mg: ασαφ a₂ Syr.: σαφαν jv Eth.: σαφατ ANhᵇnyz) ἐπὶ τῆς πατριᾶς.

Zboc₂e₂ + pauci: Ελιαβ υἱὸς Ιωαβ (ιωαδ b) ἐπὶ τῆς στρατιᾶς (vel στρατείας).

La.:   Eliab filius Ioab super patrias.

To get a full picture it is necessary on this occasion to take two items from Misc. 2 and two from the main Greek text for comparison with the single item taken from the MT. All these items deal with the same office; but it is plain that the varying textual traditions have arisen not simply from some scribal aberrations but from thoroughgoing disagreements over the question who was Army-commander under Solomon.

Let us take the main Greek text first. Here the B-tradition (represented by Bva₂ Eth.) has no Army-commander at all, for in 4: 4 it simply has a blank, and in 4: 6, where the Lucianics have an officer who was ἐπὶ τῆς στρατιᾶς, its counterpart is styled ἐπὶ τῆς πατριᾶς. But the absence of the Army-commander from this list cannot surely be a feature of the original Hebrew, even if it were of the original Greek: it is secondary, whether accidental or deliberate.

The A-tradition, in 4: 4, has Benaiah as Army-commander, but is evidently under hexaplaric influence, and cannot claim to represent the original Greek. In 4: 6 it has an officer ἐπὶ τῆς πατριᾶς (not στρατιᾶς).

The Lucianics (Zboc₂e₂) contradict themselves: in 4: 4 they have Benaiah, son of Jehoiada,[40] as Army-commander; but in 4: 6 they also have Joab's son, Eliab, as ἐπὶ τῆς στρατιᾶς. So their text, as it now stands, cannot represent the original Hebrew. Significant is the difference between its two translations: 4: 4 ἐπὶ τῆς δυνάμεως, 4: 6 ἐπὶ τῆς στρατιᾶς. Throughout the Books of Reigns the Lucianics prefer the noun στρατιά in these contexts, even when the majority text uses δύναμις (e.g. 2 Reigns 10: 7, 16; 17: 25; 19: 13 (14); 20: 23; 4 Reigns 17: 16; 21: 3, 5; 23: 4, 5). Their use of στρατιά in 4: 6 therefore is normal; their use of δύναμις in 4: 4 is abnormal (and the more surprising when the A-text uses στρατιά) and suggests that their whole phrase is a later addition, though not from the same source as the A-text's addition. If this is so, it would account for the above-mentioned contradiction in the names given for the Army-commander.

But even so we cannot accept the Lucianics' version of 4: 6 as representing the original Greek. Admittedly, all the traditions seem to agree on the officer's name, Eliab, and this may possibly represent the original Greek. But the Lucianics' patronymic, son of Joab, is altogether different from anything which the other witnesses (except the Old Latin) have, and what is more, it agrees with the patronymic given by Misc. 2. Thus it is at once suspect; moreover, even if Misc. 2's patronymic could be thought original, the Lucianics do not agree with its name for the officer: it has Αβι, whereas they in their version both of Misc. 2 and of the main text have Ελιαβ. The Lucianics, then, are a sorry mixture.[41]

Furthermore, their description of the office, in 4: 6, as ἐπὶ τῆς στρατιᾶς, as against ἐπὶ τῆς πατριᾶς of the majority, is not completely above suspicion. Montgomery (*ICC Kings*, p. 119) was sure it was original, and that πατριᾶς was a corruption of it; and maybe he was right. Certainly it would be difficult to make sense out of an office 'Over-the-Family'; yet two small pieces of evidence seem to suggest that this description of the office may be intentional. First, the office is mentioned immediately after that of the Majordomo: καὶ Αχιηλ οἰκονόμος καὶ Ελιαβ υἱὸς Σαφ ἐπὶ τῆς πατριᾶς.[42] Secondly, and more significantly, the office ἐπὶ τῆς πατριᾶς is one that does occur elsewhere in the LXX. In 1 Chron. 11: 25, among the outstanding mighty men to whom David gave high positions, we read of one whom David set ἐπὶ τὴν πατριὰν αὐτοῦ. Admittedly πατριάν is a mistaken translation, or a misreading of מִשְׁמַעְתּוֹ as if it were מִשְׁפַּחְתּוֹ; and admittedly the αὐτοῦ is ambiguous: it could mean either David's, or the mighty man's, family. But curiously enough, the mighty man in question is none other than Benaiah the son of Jehoiada, who is the storm centre of all the disagreements in the item in 3 Reigns which we are presently discussing.

It is just possible, then, that the true reading in 4: 6 is Ελιαβ υἱὸς Σαφ ἐπὶ τῆς πατριᾶς, in which case the list in the main Greek text is devoid of an Army-commander; but even if the true reading is ἐπὶ τῆς στρατιᾶς, and the list therefore manages to have an Army-commander, the most significant thing of all we have so far discussed is that the Army-commander is an otherwise unheard of Eliab and not Benaiah son of Jehoiada. After all, the main Greek text at 2: 35 follows the MT in the explicit statement that 'the king appointed Benaiah son of Jehoiada as head of the army in his [i.e. Joab's] place'. Why then does the main Greek text in ch. 4 either omit Benaiah and the office of Army-commander altogether, or else give the office to someone else?

The main Greek text itself offers no hint at its reason, but it is possible that Misc. 2 does. For when we look at the miscellany we find that it gives the office of Army-commander, not to Benaiah but to Abi, son of Joab, but unlike the main Greek text, it does not omit Benaiah altogether but gives him a different office: καὶ Βαναιας υἱὸς Ιωδαε ἐπὶ τῆς αὐλαρχίας καὶ ἐπὶ τοῦ πλινθείου. And so it indicates that Benaiah did not –

perhaps could not – hold this office along with that of Army-commander. Now not only is this office different from that which the MT gives him, the office concerned does not even appear either in the MT or the main Greek text of 3 Reigns 4. What office is it, and where has Misc. 2 got the information from? And why does it give him this office and not that of Army-commander?

The obvious place to look for answers is the lists of the king's officers that are given elsewhere. For Solomon's reign there are no other lists, but for David's reign we have several. In 2 Samuel Benaiah, son of Jehoiada, appears consistently as commander of the Cherethites and Pelethites or in connection with them (so MT 2 Sam. 8: 18; 20: 23). So also he appears in the succession narrative in 1 Kings 1: 38, 44. The Cherethites and Pelethites seem to have been the king's own personal army.[43] Both they and their commander remained loyal to David during Absalom's rebellion and to Solomon during Adonijah's attempted coup. It was natural, then, that Benaiah as their commander should be charged by Solomon with the execution of Joab and Shimei (1 Kings 2: 29–34 and 46) and that upon Joab's execution Solomon should appoint the loyal Benaiah commander-in-chief of the national army (1 Kings 2: 35).

So far everything is simple and eminently credible; and it is difficult to see why Misc. 2 should come up with the far less credible story that Solomon appointed Joab's son as Army-commander.[44] But complications begin to set in when 1 Chron. 27: 5–6 seems to say that this military commander, Benaiah, was a priest: 'The third captain of the host for the third month was Benaiah, the son of Jehoiada, the priest, chief...This is that Benaiah who was the mighty man of the Thirty, and over the Thirty...' Admittedly the Hebrew could as well, perhaps could better, be taken as the NEB takes it: 'Third, Benaiah the son of Jehoiada the chief priest, commander of the army,...' (i.e. Jehoiada was the chief priest),[45] but the Greek understands Benaiah to be the priest: Βαναιας ὁ τοῦ Ιωδαε ὁ ἱερεὺς ὁ ἄρχων, the case usage putting the matter beyond dispute.

There is, of course, no real difficulty in Benaiah's being called
a priest, for the priesthood in question was not the Levitical
priesthood, nor was the office sacerdotal.[46] 'Priest' here is used
in the sense which it has in 2 Sam. 8: 18 'And David's sons
were priests', i.e. some kind of court official. Some Greek
translations, moreover, have well understood this meaning of
the term 'priest'. The Greek of this passage in 2 Sam. 8: 18, for
instance, is: υἱοὶ Δαυιδ αὐλάρχαι ἦσαν. On the other hand the
Hebrew of the counterpart passage in Chronicles (1 Chron.
18: 17) has felt it necessary to remove any possible misunderstanding by rephrasing it: the sons of David were הָרִאשֹׁנִים
לְיַד הַמֶּלֶךְ. It could be, therefore, that Misc. 2 also felt a difficulty
over Benaiah's priesthood: taking it in the Levitical sense, it
has regarded it as being incompatible with the office of Army-
commander and therefore has decided that Benaiah could not
have been Army-commander.

To have any cogency this suggestion would need, of course, to
be able to show that the office which Misc. 2 does assign to
Benaiah was not likewise incompatible with priesthood. The
office is described as ἐπὶ τῆς αὐλαρχίας καὶ ἐπὶ τοῦ πλινθείου.
What does this mean? The fact that there are two terms recalls
that in the lists of David's ministers and elsewhere Benaiah is
consistently represented as having been 'over the Cherethites
and the Pelethites'. Maybe, then, ἐπὶ τῆς αὐλαρχίας καὶ ἐπὶ τοῦ
πλινθείου is offered as a (mistaken, or far-fetched) translation
of 'over the Cherethites and the Pelethites'. If so, rabbinic
exegesis would not have regarded this office as incompatible
with priesthood. Consider, for example, the reading of B s h at
1 Chron. 18: 17. For the MT's 'And Benaiah the son of
Jehoiada was over the Cherethites and the Pelethites', while
the majority of Greek manuscripts have καὶ Βαναιας υἱὸς
Ιωδαε ἐπὶ τοῦ Χερεθθι καὶ τοῦ Φελεθθι, B s h have Βαναιας υἱος
Ιωδαε ἐπὶ τῶν ἱερέων καὶ Φαλτεια; and the Lucianics, be$_2$,
agree with them at least in having ἐπὶ τῶν ἱερέων.[47] So here all
the Cherethites have become priests!

Later rabbinical exegesis, on the other hand, turned the
Cherethites and Pelethites into the Sanhedrin, and Benaiah

into the President of the Sanhedrin and/or a Levitical priest. Take, for instance, the Babylonian Talmud,[48] *Sanhedrin*, 16a–b. It is discussing the Mishnah: 'War of free choice can be waged only by the authority of a court of seventy-one.' It begins by arguing thus:

Whence do we deduce this? – Said R. Abbahu: Scripture states, *And he shall stand before Eleazar the Priest (who shall inquire for him by the judgement of the Urim before the Lord. At his word they shall go out and at his word they shall come in, both he and all the children of Israel with him, even all the Congregation).* '*He*', refers to the King; '*And all the children of Israel with him*', to the Priest anointed for the conduct of the war; and '*all the Congregation*', means the Sanhedrin. But perhaps it is the Sanhedrin whom the Divine Law instructs to inquire of the *Urim* and *Tummim*? But (it may be deduced) from the story related by R. Aha b. Bizna in the name of R. Simeon the Pious:...David said...Go and stretch forth your hands with a troop (of soldiers)! Immediately they held counsel with Ahitophel and took advice from the Sanhedrin and inquired of the *Urim* and *Tummim*. R. Joseph said: What passage (states this)? – *And after Ahitophel was Benaiah the son of Jehoiada*[49] *and Abiathar; and the Captain of the king's host was Joab*. '*Ahitophel*' is the adviser, even as it is written, *And the counsel of Ahitophel which he counselled in those days, was as if a man inquired from the word of God*. '*Benaiah the son of Jehoiada*', refers to the Sanhedrin, and '*Abiathar*' to the *Urim* and *Tummim*. And so it is written, *And Benaiah the son of Jehoiada was over the Kerethites and Pelethites*. And why were they termed *Kerethites*? – Because they gave definite instructions.[50] And *Pelethites*? – Because their acts were wonderful.[51] Only after this (is it written), *And the captain of the king's host was Joab*.[52]

The validity of exegesis that can turn the Cherethites and Pelethites into the Sanhedrin is, of course, not under discussion here; we should simply notice that this piece of exegesis spread and developed variations,[53] and among them the idea that Benaiah was a *Levitical* priest. In consequence other exegetes denied that this Benaiah was identical with his namesake, the commander-in-chief of Solomon's army.[54] Their reason seems to have been that the Benaiah who was Army-commander acted as an executioner (1 Kings 2: 34, 46), which work would contravene the laws of Levitical purity, and therefore cannot have been performed by the Benaiah who was both Head of the Sanhedrin (the Cherethites and Pelethites) and a (Levitical) priest. Now all this, of course, is much later than the Septuagint, so that the most we could say would be that Misc. 2's treatment of Benaiah's office shows an early stage of the misgivings and speculations which later rabbis revelled in. But so far we have only surmised that the ἐπὶ τῆς αὐλαρχίας καὶ ἐπὶ τοῦ πλινθείου of Misc. 2 may have been a (mis)translation of 'over the Cherethites and the Pelethites'; in actual fact this surmise, though possible, is by no means certain; and deciphering the meaning of the phrase is not at all straightforward.

Αὐλαρχία, in the first element of the phrase, is not a common word in the Septuagint: this is, indeed, its only occurrence. The related word αὐλάρχης likewise occurs only once, in 2 Sam. 8: 18 υἱοὶ Δαυιδ αὐλάρχαι ἦσαν. Interestingly enough, αὐλάρχαι here stands, as we have seen,[55] for the MT כֹּהֲנִים 'priests'. If, then, as seems probable, the αὐλαρχία of Misc. 2 is in some way related, as a translation, to the αὐλάρχαι of 2 Sam. 8: 18, it still connects Benaiah, indirectly, at least, with the idea of priesthood of some kind; but it can hardly be intended at the same time as a direct translation of עַל־הַכְּרֵתִי 'over the Cherethites'.

Πλινθεῖον, in the second element of the phrase, presents further difficulties. It seems practically certain that it has some connection with the rendering offered by the Lucianics in 2 Sam. 20: 23. There, instead of the majority reading which describes Benaiah's office as ἐπὶ τοῦ Χερεθθι καὶ ἐπὶ τοῦ Φελεθθι, the Lucianics, boc₂e₂ z(mg) Thdt, have ἐπὶ τοῦ πλινθίου καὶ ἐπὶ τοὺς δυναστάς (δυνάτους Thdt) while the Old Latin has *desuper lateris* (-*res* La.[2]) *et in ponentibus*. Now δυνατὸς is the regular translation of גִּבֹּרִים in 2 Sam., though boc₂e₂ consistently prefer δυνάσται (see, e.g. 2 Sam. 23: 8). So ἐπὶ τῶν δυναστῶν (-ατων) is not a strict translation of עַל־הַפְּלֵתִי, but a paraphrase. In that case, ἐπὶ τοῦ πλινθίου may well not be a strict translation of עַל־הַכְּרֵתִי, but only a paraphrase. Now there are two or three possible meanings of πλινθίου. It could be an itacism for πλινθείου 'brickworks'. The word occurs a few chapters earlier, 2 Sam. 12: 31, where among the things which David did to the conquered Ammonites was this: διήγαγεν αὐτοὺς διὰ τοῦ πλινθείου. Here however the Lucianics do not use the word πλινθεῖον but have simply a transliteration ἐν μαδεββα (vel sim.). Shall we then say that πλινθίου is not an itacism,[46] but the genitive of πλινθίον, used in the same sense as πλαίσιον, 'a square of troops'? Theodoret, who follows the Lucianic text, thought that this was its meaning (*Quaestiones in II Reg.*, XL).[57] Whichever meaning we prefer, however, it does seem that πλινθ(ε)ιου is not a translation but an interpretative paraphrase. On the other hand, the fact that the Lucianics have a double expression ἐπὶ τοῦ πλινθ(ε)ιου καὶ ἐπὶ τοὺς δυνάστας shows that their paraphrase is meant to be the equivalent of the double expression in the Hebrew, 'over the Cherethites and the Pelethites'.

If, then, ἐπὶ τοῦ πλινθείου in Misc. 2 is based on, or agrees with, the Lucianic version in 2 Sam. 20: 23, it is, in origin, a remote equivalent of 'over the Cherethites'. Yet strangely enough ἐπὶ τοῦ πλινθείου in Misc. 2 is the *second* element in the phrase, and not the first as it is in the Lucianic paraphrase. Moreover the *first* element in the phrase in Misc. 2, ἐπὶ τῆς αὐλαρχίας seems, as we have noticed above (p. 88), to be an equivalent not of 'over the Cherethites', not even of 'over the Pelethites', but of something else. So we cannot say that the office given to Benaiah by Misc. 2 is the equivalent of 'over the Cherethites and the Pelethites'. It is an uneasy mixture, going back eventually to a Hebrew something like 'over the priests (court-officials) and the Cherethites'. But the fact that it is an uneasy mixture suggests that it is not an attempt at a strict translation of a Hebrew text, but an editor's collection of some interpretative paraphrases. How much additional rabbinic 'meaning' the editor may have read into these paraphrases we cannot say. What we can say as a result of this long discussion is that the debate over the office held by Benaiah began in very early times, and soon became complicated and confused; and that it was as a result of this debate that both Misc. 2 and the main Greek text at 4: 1–6 denied to Benaiah the office of Army-commander (although the main Greek text at 2: 35 and the MT at both 2: 35 and 4: 4 assigned the office to him), and that Misc. 2 substituted an office compiled, with no great accuracy, out of earlier interpretative paraphrases.

Item 6

MT   וְצָדוֹק וְאֶבְיָתָר כֹּהֲנִים

Misc. 2   Nil (but cf. Item 1: Αζαριου υἰὸς Σαδωκ τοῦ ἰερέως)

MGT   καὶ Σαδουχ καὶ Αβιαθαρ ἱερεῖς

We have already discussed this item in connection with Item 2
(see p. 78). Within the limits of this Item 6 the main Greek text
agrees fully with the MT; the miscellany disagrees totally.

Item 7

MT   וַעֲזַרְיָהוּ בֶן־נָתָן עַל־הַנִּצָּבִים

Misc. 2   καὶ Ορνιου υἰὸς Ναθαν ἄρχων τῶν ἐφεστηκότων

MGT   καὶ Ορνια υἰὸς Ναθαν ἐπὶ τῶν καθεσταμένων

Neither Misc. 2 nor the main Greek text agrees with the MT
fully – over the officer's name they are nearer to each other
than either is to the MT.[58] The ἐπὶ of the main Greek text is
closer to the עַל of the MT than is the ἄρχων of Misc. 2, which
could be based on a Hebrew text which read שַׂר, or could
simply be a more idiomatic translation of the MT. If there is
any real difference in the terms ἐφεστηκότων and καθεσταμένων, the former would emphasise that the men whom Ορνιου
controlled were themselves overseers, while the latter indicates
merely that they were 'appointed officials'. In the Books of
Reigns the participle ἐφεστηκώς does not elsewhere occur in
this sense; καθεσταμένοι is the normal term. On the other hand
it does occur in other books, e.g. Judith 12: 11.

Item 8

MT   וְזָבוּד בֶּן־נָתָן כֹּהֵן רֵעֶה הַמֶּלֶךְ

Misc. 2   καὶ Ζαχουρ υἰὸς Ναθαν ὁ σύμβουλος

MGT   καὶ Ζαβουθ υἰὸς Ναθαν ἑταῖρος τοῦ βασιλέως

The difference Ζαχουρ/Ζαβουθ goes back to variants in the
Hebrew manuscripts: several Hebrew manuscripts read וזכור.
The main Greek text agrees with the MT's reading. Similarly
in the description of the office: the ἑταῖρος τοῦ βασιλέως of the

main text agrees exactly with the MT; the ὁ σύμβουλος of
Misc. 2 does not. While 'Royal Friend' is a well known title, it
is perfectly possible that Misc. 2 should have had a Hebrew
vorlage that read יוֹעֵץ (cf. 2 Sam. 15: 12). On the other hand,
it could be an 'explanatory' translation. When, for instance, in
2 Sam. 8: 18 the MT mistakenly has 'Benaiah the son of
Jehoiada *and* the Cherethites and Pelethites' instead of the
normal '...*over* the Cherethites and Pelethites', the Greek has
'Benaiah the son of Jehoiada σύμβουλος and the Cherethites
and Pelethites'. Here σύμβουλος has every appearance of a
convenient word put in to try and plug the gap caused by the
mistake. Again, Hushai the Archite, who in 2 Sam. 15: 32 is
called both by the MT and the LXX 'Friend of the King' was
in fact David's most famous 'Counsellor'. It could well be
therefore that ὁ σύμβουλος in Misc. 2 is simply an alternative
translation meant to explain what office 'Friend-of-the-King'
was. Certainly when boc₂e₂ dp La. offer as a variant of ὁ
σύμβουλος the translation ἐν τοῖς συμβούλοις, theirs is an
explanatory translation to make it clear that Ζαχουρ was not
the sole Counsellor, but one among many.

Item 9

MT   וַאֲחִישָׁר עַל־הַבָּיִת
Misc. 2   καὶ Εδραμ ἐπὶ τὸν οἶκον αὐτοῦ
MGT   καὶ Αχιηλ οἰκονόμος[59]

In the main Greek text A with the majority reads Αχισαρ.
B reads Αχει ἦν which would seem to be a simple corruption of
an original Αχιηλ, which is the reading of the Lucianics.[60] It
would, of course, have been very easy for a translator to misread
שָׂר עַל־הַבָּיִת וַאֲחִישָׁר עַל as וַאֲחִי שָׂר עַל and then to have translated
as ἦν οἰκονόμος. But whichever reading is original, Αχι, Αχιηλ,
or Αχισαρ, they are all nearer the MT than is Εδραμ of Misc.
2. On the other hand, the ἐπὶ τὸν οἶκον αὐτοῦ of Misc. 2 is a
more literal translation of the Hebrew than is the οἰκονόμος
of the main Greek text. The significance of this, however,
is by no means certain, since in 2 Kings – to take just one

example – עַל־הַבַּיִת is rendered both by ἐπὶ τῷ οἴκῳ (15: 5) and by οἰκονόμος (18: 18); the variation could be simply stylistic.

Item 10

MT   וַאֲדֹנִירָם בֶּן־עַבְדָּא עַל־הַמַּס

Misc. 2   καὶ Αχιρε[61] υἱὸς Εδραϊ[62] ἐπὶ τὰς ἄρσεις

MGT   καὶ Αδωνιραμ υἱὸς Εφρα[63] ἐπὶ τῶν φόρων

Over the officer's name the main Greek text agrees with the MT, Misc. 2 does not. Over the patronymic neither Misc. 2 nor the main Greek text agrees with the MT. In the name of the office the term מַס is regularly translated φόρος (normally in the singular) in Judges, Samuel, Kings[64] and Chronicles, whereas ἄρσις seems nowhere else to be used for מַס throughout the whole OT. What ἄρσις is normally used for is סֵבֶל or סַבָּל (or else, in a different sense, for מַשָּׂא vel sim.). The point of using it here, therefore, is not clear.

In connection with the variation in the names it is interesting to notice the wide difference in the Lucianic manuscripts (see footnotes 61–3, page 127). These can hardly all be mere scribal errors; and it would seem, therefore, that for some reason now no longer discernible, there must have been some debate over this officer.

With this we have completed our examination of all Solomon's ministers. The result has been to show that text-wise this section of the miscellany is generally further off the MT than is the main Greek text; and this is true also for the order in which the items are placed. But the main text is by no means closely conformed to the MT; sometimes it is not so near as the miscellany is, and at other times it is nearer to the miscellany than it is to the MT. Some differences are merely scribal, of course, but several are occasioned by variations in the underlying Hebrew texts, while the most important arise from debate over the meaning and implication of the original Hebrew text. In other words, the mixture is the same as in the other sections of the miscellanies.

CHAPTER 6

AN INTERESTING ADDITION
TO THE SECOND MISCELLANY

Verse g of Misc. 2 ends in this way: 'and Judah and Israel dwelt securely, each man under his vine and under his fig tree, eating and drinking from Dan to Beersheba all the days of Solomon.' But in the Lucianics there occurs the following addition:

πάσας τὰς ἡμέρας Σαλωμων] πασας τας ημερας σολομωντος και ουκ ην σαταν πασας τας ημερας σολομωντος Z (vid.) boc₂e₂ dgp ⟦πασας τας ημερας] πασαις ταις ημεραις Z (vid.): εν ταις ημεραις be₂ | (other small variants)⟧.

There is no reason to think that this reading of the Lucianics is an original reading that has in all other manuscripts fallen out as a result of parablepsis (σολομωντος^{1o} ∩ σολομωντος^{2o}). In several other instances (see above, pp. 82ff.), the peculiar readings of the Lucianics in the miscellanies have every appearance of later refinements. But this particular instance is worth a brief study as an example of the processes by which the miscellanies, once formed, tended to grow.

The source of this additional information that 'there was no adversary all the days of Solomon' is doubtless a Hebrew text like that of MT 1 Kings 5: 18 (EVV 5: 4):[1] אֵין שָׂטָן וְאֵין פֶּגַע רָע. The main Greek text *in loco* (Rahlfs 5: 18; BM 5: 4) has οὐκ ἔστι ἐπίβουλος καὶ οὐκ ἔστιν ἀπάντημα (ἁμάρτημα Ba₂) πονηρόν. Only part of this information, however, appears in the miscellany, and that part is differently translated, and has an addition calculated to make it fit its context.

It is easy to see, first of all, the reason for fitting this information into its present position in the miscellany. V. g begins: 'And there was peace to him on all sides round about, and Judah and Israel dwelt securely...'[2] The verse from which the additional information comes (5: 18) expresses a similar sentiment: 'But

93

now the Lord my God has given me rest on every side; there is
neither adversary...' The themes being similar, the phrase
'there was no adversary...' would naturally occur to the mind
under the prompting of v. g, though the strict equivalent of
v. g in the MT is not 5: 18, but 5: 4.

Secondly, the phrase πάσας τὰς ἡμέρας Σολομῶντος has
been added to the additional clause in the miscellany, simply in
order to make it fit better on to the end of v. g which itself ends
πάσας τὰς ἡμέρας Σαλωμων. But this little piece of textual
adaptation has betrayed the miscellany into an exaggeration
which, while it sounds well enough within the context of the
miscellany itself, flatly contradicts the facts as given by the main
Greek text at 11: 4: καὶ ἤγειρεν Κύριος σαταν τῷ Σαλωμων...
καὶ ἦσαν σαταν τῷ Ισραηλ πάσας τὰς ἡμέρας Σαλωμων. It
seems unlikely that the contradiction was intentional.

Most interesting of all is the difference in translation,
ἐπίβουλος/σαταν, between the main Greek text at 5: 18 and
v. g of the miscellany.[3] Doubtless σαταν is a much more
literalistic translation – a transliteration, in fact; yet it stands in
the miscellany, while the more idiomatic ἐπίβουλος stands in the
main text. On the other hand v. g of the miscellany differs
substantially from MT 1 Kings 5: 18, while the main text at
that point agrees with the MT fully. So one can neither argue
that the miscellany here is more idiomatic than the main text
and therefore earlier, nor that it is more closely conformed to
MT and therefore later. In fact, while the main text uses the
idiomatic ἐπίβουλος at 5: 18, it itself uses the transliteration
σαταν, as we have seen, at 11: 14. So the variation ἐπίβουλος/
σαταν is not necessarily in itself an indication of difference of
translator. On the other hand at 2 Sam. 19: 22 (33), where the
majority text reads ἐπίβουλον, a substantial minority[4] has
σαταν, and this, presumably, does arise from a difference of
translator. The transliteration σαταν must, of course, go back
to some Hebrew שָׂטָן; but whether σαταν in the Lucianics'
addition in Misc. 2 is based directly on this Hebrew, or whether
some later editor has borrowed it from some other Greek translation, who can say?

The addition, then, is in itself unimportant; but the uncertainties that surround its source are a healthy reminder of the complications that beset the task of unravelling the many strands that go to make up the 'Lucianic' text as presented by boc_2e_2 in the Book of Reigns.

CHAPTER 7

THE DUPLICATE PART I
OF THE SHIMEI STORY

Pt IA. Main Greek text (Rahlfs): 2: 8–9 = MT 2: 8–9.

8 καὶ ἰδοῦ μετὰ σοῦ Σεμεϊ υἱὸς Γηρα υἱὸς τοῦ Ιεμενι ἐκ Βαουριμ, καὶ αὐτὸς κατηράσατό με κατάραν ὀδυνηρὰν τῇ ἡμέρᾳ, ᾗ ἐπορευόμην εἰς Παρεμβολάς, καὶ αὐτὸς κατέβη εἰς ἀπαντήν μου εἰς τὸν Ιορδάνην, καὶ ὤμοσα αὐτῷ ἐν κυρίῳ λέγων Εἰ θανατώσω σε ἐν ῥομφαίᾳ· 9 καὶ οὐ μὴ ἀθῳώσῃς αὐτόν, ὅτι ἀνὴρ σοφὸς εἶ σὺ καὶ γνώσῃ ἃ ποιήσεις αὐτῷ, καὶ κατάξεις τὴν πολιὰν αὐτοῦ ἐν αἵματι εἰς ᾅδου.

Pt IB. ?Main Greek text or Misc. 2 (Rahlfs): 2: 35^{1-o} = MT 2: 8–9.

35^1 Καὶ ἐν τῷ ἔτι Δαυιδ ζῆν ἐνετείλατο τῷ Σαλωμων λέγων Ἰδοὺ μετὰ σοῦ Σεμεϊ υἱὸς Γηρα υἱὸς σπέρματος τοῦ Ιεμινι ἐκ Χεβρων· 35^m οὗτος κατηράσατό με κατάραν ὀδυνηρὰν ἐν ᾗ ἡμέρᾳ ἐπορευόμην εἰς Παρεμβολάς, 35^n καὶ αὐτὸς κατέβαινεν εἰς ἀπαντήν μοι ἐπὶ τὸν Ιορδάνην, καὶ ὤμοσα αὐτῷ κατὰ τοῦ κυρίου λέγων Εἰ θανατωθήσεται ἐν ῥομφαίᾳ· 35° καὶ νῦν μὴ ἀθῳώσῃς αὐτόν, ὅτι ἀνὴρ φρόνιμος σὺ καὶ γνώσῃ ἃ ποιήσεις αὐτῷ, καὶ κατάξεις τὴν πολιὰν αὐτοῦ ἐν αἵματι εἰς ᾅδου.

We have now completed our investigation of the two miscellanies, but before we attempt to sum up our findings, we must consider briefly the related phenomenon of the duplicate Part IA and Part IB of the story of Shimei. The necessity is laid upon us by the fact that the two miscellanies are grouped before and after the Shimei story thus:

Misc. 1	2: 35^{a-k}
Shimei Pt IB	35^{1-o} = MT 2: 8–9
Shimei Pt II	36–46 = MT 2: 36–46
Misc. 2	46^{a-1}

and by the other fact that the translation, Shimei Pt IB, has no

96

counterpart in the MT in this position. In this latter respect, therefore, it resembles many of the items in the two miscellanies which surround it; and this in turn raises the question, whether Pt IB is to be regarded as part of the main Greek text or part of (or an addendum to) the miscellanies.

There is moreover a further resemblance between the miscellanies and this doublet Pt IB: both miscellanies are artificially and deliberately contrived in order to stress, and give examples of, Solomon's wisdom.[1] Now the story of Shimei and his execution furnishes another example of Solomon's wisdom, but it is Pt I of the story that explicitly mentions that fact.[2] If, then, the miscellanies had been grouped simply around Pt II of the Shimei story, the connection between their 'wisdom-theme' and Pt II would not have been apparent; with Pt IB in its present position, the connection is explicit.

This means no more, however, than that Pt IB is necessary to the scheme of the two miscellanies; the two miscellanies are not necessary to Pt IB. Or, to put it in other words, Pt IB could have stood in its present position in the text and made perfect sense before the miscellanies were added; they, on the other hand, seem to need the presence of Pt IB to make their positioning in the text intelligible. And this seems to mean that Pt IB was either in the text before the miscellanies were added, and so was part of the main Greek text; or that Pt IB was added simultaneously with the miscellanies by the editor of the miscellanies, and so was part of the miscellanies; but that Pt IB was not added *after* the miscellanies – which piece of evidence unfortunately does not go far towards solving our problem.

Let us try another tack. Let us compare the translations in Pt IA and Pt IB to see if they are from the same hand or from different hands; and if either of them shows marks of being a later translation or of having suffered revision; and if Pt IB has any interpretative elements in it such as we have found in the miscellanies.

	Pt IA	Pt IB	MT
1		καὶ ἐν τῷ ἔτι Δαυιδ ʒῆν	
		ἐνετείλατο τῷ Σ. λέγων	
2	καὶ ἰδοὺ μετά σου	Ἰδοὺ μετὰ σοῦ	וְהִנֵּה עִמְּךָ
3	Σεμεΐ υἱὸς Γηρα	Σεμεΐ υἱὸς Γηρα	שִׁמְעִי בֶן־גֵּרָא
4	υἱὸς	υἱὸς σπέρματος	בֶּן־
5	τοῦ Ιεμενι	τοῦ Ιεμινι	הַיְמִינִי
6	ἐκ Βαουριμ	ἐκ Χεβρων	מִבַּחֻרִים
7	καὶ αὐτὸς	οὗτος	וְהוּא
8	κατηράσατό με	κατηράσατό με	קִלְלַנִי
9	κατάραν ὀδυνηρὰν	κατάραν ὀδυνηρὰν	קְלָלָה נִמְרֶצֶת
10	τῇ ἡμέρᾳ ᾗ	ἐν ᾗ ἡμέρᾳ	בְּיוֹם
11	ἐπορευόμην εἰς	ἐπορευόμην εἰς	לֶכְתִּי מַחֲנָיִם
	Παρεμβολάς	Παρεμβολάς	
12	καὶ αὐτὸς κατέβη	καὶ αὐτὸς κατέβαινεν	וְהוּא יָרַד
13	εἰς ἀπαντήν μου	εἰς ἀπαντήν μοι	לִקְרָאתִי
14	εἰς τὸν Ιορδάνην	ἐπὶ τὸν Ιορδάνην	הַיַּרְדֵּן
15	καὶ ὤμοσα αὐτῷ	καὶ ὤμοσα αὐτῷ	וָאֶשָּׁבַע לוֹ
16	ἐν κυρίῳ λέγων	κατὰ τοῦ κυρίου λέγων	בַיהוה לֵאמֹר
17	Εἰ θανατώσω σε	Εἰ θανατωθήσεται	אִם־אֲמִיתְךָ
18	ἐν ῥομφαίᾳ	ἐν ῥομφαίᾳ	בֶּחָרֶב:
19	καὶ οὐ	καὶ νῦν	וְעַתָּה
20	μὴ ἀθωώσῃς αὐτόν	μὴ ἀθωώσῃς αὐτόν	אַל־תְּנַקֵּהוּ
21	ὅτι ἀνὴρ σοφὸς	ὅτι ἀνὴρ φρόνιμος	כִּי אִישׁ חָכָם
22	εἶ σὺ	σὺ	אָתָּה
23	καὶ γνώσῃ	καὶ γνώσῃ	וְיָדַעְתָּ
24	ἃ ποιήσεις αὐτῷ	ἃ ποιήσεις αὐτῷ	אֵת אֲשֶׁר תַּעֲשֶׂה־לּוֹ
25	καὶ κατάξεις	καὶ κατάξεις	וְהוֹרַדְתָּ
26	τὴν πολιὰν αὐτοῦ	τὴν πολιὰν αὐτοῦ	אֶת־שֵׂיבָתוֹ
27	ἐν αἵματι εἰς ᾅδου	ἐν αἵματι εἰς ᾅδου	בְּדָם שְׁאוֹל

There are three major differences between Pt IA and Pt IB:
items 1, 4 and 6. Of them, item 1 is an introductory explanation
made necessary by the position of Pt IB in the text; it also
necessarily involves the absence of καὶ from item 2. In itself
therefore this difference would not necessarily indicate a difference of translator. The other two major differences, how-

ever, are more significant and seem to imply a different hand: υἱὸς σπέρματος (item 4) is a doublet with υἱὸς Γηρα (item 3) and goes back to בֶּן־גֵּרָא read as בֶּן־זֶרַע. It could be a later gloss on the correct and original υἱὸς Γηρα; or it could be the original, mistaken translation and υἱὸς Γηρα a later correction. In item 6 Χεβρων is not only different from Βαουριμ, but, in view of the events to which it refers (related in 2 Sam. 16: 5, 19: 16), it is most unlikely geographically. It is possible, perhaps, that it arose from a misreading of מבחרים as if it were מחברון; but Hebron is so famous as David's first capital city, and it would therefore be so odd for Shimei, a relative of Saul, to come from Hebron, that one would have expected a translator who fell into such a misreading to realise his mistake at once and to correct it. Perhaps there is some deliberate, but fanciful, midrashic interpretation involved.

At any rate, in these three major differences it is Pt IA each time that is the nearer to the MT. In four other, small variants, items 7, 13, 16 and 17, Pt IA is nearer to the MT than Pt IB is, and is the more literalistic for it.

On the other hand, in two instances, nos. 19 and 22, it is Pt IB that is the nearer to the MT; though in no. 19 the Lucianic manuscripts read καὶ σὺ οὐ, and σὺ/οὐ may be a doublet in which σὺ is the original reading, going back to a different Hebrew – אַתָּה instead of עַתָּה.

Four items, nos. 5, 10, 12, 14, concern small matters of style or orthography; a fifth, which might well come under this head, is claimed by some as more significant: for the Hebrew חָכָם (item 21) Pt IB uses φρόνιμος, which Montgomery[3] and Shenkel[4] claim as a mark of the Old Greek, while Pt IA uses σοφός which is claimed by Montgomery as a later translation, and by Shenkel as a mark of the 'kaige' recension. In this connection item 13 is also interesting. Barthélemy claims[5] that the phrase εἰς ἀπαντήν is recensional, as distinct from the original (or a subsequent reversion to the original) εἰς ἀπάντησιν. About half the manuscripts read εἰς ἀπαντήν in Pt IA;[6] and this would support the view that Pt IA has come under revision. In Pt IB only Ba₂ read εἰς ἀπαντήν. If this is the true reading, as Rahlfs seems to think, then all the others, which have εἰς ἀπάντησιν, must be later reversions to more natural Greek. It could be, however, that Ba₂ are simply under the influence of the form used in Pt IA, and have not been affected directly by the 'kaige' recension.

To be put against these differences are 12 items (nos. 3, 8, 9, 11, 15, 18, 20, 23–7) in which Pt IA and Pt IB are exactly alike. Some of this agreement may, of course, be merely coincidental; but items 8–9 show an agreement which, if it is coincidental, is remarkable: ὀδυνηρός is a rare word in the LXX, occurring only four times apart from these two instances; that both Pt IA and Pt IB use it suggests interdependence.

Now what theory will cover all, or most, of these phenomena? To start with, the combination of extensive basic similarity coupled with several small literalistic translations in Pt IA that bring it nearer to the MT, suggests that Pt IA has undergone a revision – perhaps the 'kaige' revision – which Pt IB has not.

But to say that Pt IA has been revised by the 'kaige' recension implies that Pt IA already stood in the text *before* the revision took place, and that its position, as distinct from its present form, is very early, if not original. But this leads us up against a problem. If Pt IA already stood in its position when the rest of 3 Reigns was being translated, surely no translator, unless his Hebrew text compelled him to it, would have inserted Pt IB to repeat what Pt IA had already said only a few lines before. Nor surely would any subsequent reviser. Still less would either of them have introduced the insertion with an explanation 'And while David still lived he charged Solomon saying', if a few lines earlier Pt IA had already made this precise point explicitly.

Are we then to think that when Pt IB was translated, Pt IA was not yet present in the text? This could be, if we assume that 3 Reigns, including Pt IB, was based on a Hebrew text in which the introductory verses to the Shimei story stood not where the MT has them but where Pt IB has them. Then we should have to assume that the 'kaige' recension came along, using a Hebrew text which had the verses in the MT position, and filled in

Pt IA, which hitherto had all of it been absent from this position. This would account for the fact that Pt IA is nearer the MT than Pt IB is, and for the fact that Pt IB was allowed to stay even when a more 'correct' version had been supplied in the form and position of Pt IA. But unfortunately there is a snag: the manuscripts that normally are not affected by the 'kaige' recension[7] all have Pt IA; in fact, no manuscript cited by BM lacks it. This makes it difficult to think that Pt IA was supplied (as distinct from being revised) by the 'kaige' recension.

So let us try another theory. Up till now we have been assuming that Pt IA and Pt IB, once they were inserted in the Greek text, stood in the same Biblical book (3 Reigns) within a few inches of each other in the same scroll. But that is not necessarily so. The Lucianic manuscripts boc_2e_2 and also the manuscripts g and v(mg) claim that 2 Reigns originally continued as far as what is now 3 Reigns 2: 11, and that 3 Reigns did not begin until 3 Reigns 2: 12. Thackeray[8] thought they were right, and Montgomery,[9] though not Rahlfs,[10] agreed; and certainly the death of David (3 Reigns 2: 11) and the accession of Solomon (3 Reigns 2: 12) make a very natural place at which to divide these two Books of Reigns. Now if the division between 2 and 3 Reigns was originally made here, and if, as is likely, 1–2 Reigns was written on one scroll and 3–4 Reigns on another, then the translator of 2 Reigns would have originally translated the introduction to the Shimei story (Pt IA), since it comes at what is now 3 Reigns 2: 8–9; and then at v. 11 the scroll would have ended. The main part of the Shimei story, coming, as it does, at what is now 3 Reigns 2: 36–46, would have been translated by the translator of 3 Reigns and would have stood in a different scroll. But since the introduction is necessary to the full understanding of the main story, it would then have been a very natural and sensible thing for the translator, or a subsequent reviser, of 3 Reigns to insert Pt IB immediately before the main story, for the benefit of readers who either had not read, or could not remember, the introduction as given by Pt IA in the separate scroll of 1–2 Reigns. Pt IA and Pt IB would no longer be repetitious.[11]

This theory would account for the basic similarity between Pt IA and Pt IB and yet for the greater nearness of Pt IA to the MT. Pt IB would have been inserted in 3 Reigns before Pt IA had undergone (along with the preceding chapters) the 'kaige' recension;[12] and it would be natural for the translator, or reviser, of 3 Reigns to look up the translation of Pt IA in 2 Reigns and to use it practically verbatim for Pt IB. The only modification it would need would be the provision at the beginning of a note (such as Pt IB now has) explaining that this charge was given to Solomon by David before David's death. The revision that subsequently conformed the second half of 2 Reigns to the MT would then have covered Pt IA; but Pt IB, which stood in 3 Reigns, would have been left as it was.[13]

Yet all this would still not tell us whether Pt IB was supplied by the translator of 3 Reigns as part of the main Greek text to which the miscellanies were later added, or whether Pt IB was added by some subsequent reviser along with the miscellanies. No definite answer can be given,[14] though a little speculation might not be entirely unprofitable. If Pt IB contained any notably midrashic element such as we have found in the miscellanies, this, though not amounting to proof, might incline the verdict towards thinking that Pt IB was part of the miscellanies.

Now Pt IB does contain two items that are so strange as to raise the possibility that they may have arisen from fanciful midrashic interpretation: they are the items 3–4 and 6. Montgomery thought them nothing but clumsy errors.[15] His words are '...the marks of the elder Greek translator...the clumsy errors characteristic of the oldest Greek, e.g. "Hebron" for "Bahurim" and υἱὸς τοῦ σπέρματος for בן גרא read as בן זרע, then glossed with a doublet'. Maybe Montgomery is right; but if they are simply errors they are certainly very clumsy errors, and it would be fairer to the original translator if we did not immediately assume gross incompetence in him, but looked around first for some excuse or for some other possible explanation.

Patronymics in Hebrew are so very common that to mistake

the proper name גֵּרָא in the patronymic בֶּן־גֵּרָא for the common noun זֶרַע, and to translate it by the tautologous 'son of the seed of' (υἱὸς τοῦ σπέρματος) would be incompetence indeed. Worse still would it be to mistake Bahurim for Hebron, particularly in the light of the history given in 2 Sam., to which Pt IB itself draws attention. That history was this: upon Absalom's rebellion David left Jerusalem and in the course of his flight came to a place, not far from Jerusalem, called Bahurim. There there met him a man from Bahurim – which was natural enough – who being a relative of Saul, cursed David – perhaps that was natural as well. On David's return towards Jerusalem this man, called Shimei, came down from Bahurim to the Jordan to meet David and implore forgiveness. Neither going or returning did David go anywhere near Hebron which not only is 19 miles S.S.W. of Jerusalem (whereas David's flight was to the N.E.), but was also at the time in the hands of Absalom who had made it the headquarters of the rebellion.

If, then, in the end we have to put 'Hebron' down to a mistake, some excuse could be found for our translator by observing that בחרים, on the few occasions it occurs in the OT, has always given[16] translators, or scribes, or both, a difficult time. In 2 Sam. 3: 16 only a few manuscripts manage to read Βαουρειμ; the majority read Βαρακει(μ) (vel sim.). In 2 Sam. 16:5 the Lucianics have Χορραμ,[17] and in 19: 16 (17) Χορραν; while in 17: 18 they have Βαιθχορρων. So the translator of Pt IB likewise may have found מבחרים difficult and, as suggested above, may have misread it as מחברון.

But the Lucianics in both Pt IB and in Pt IA have an alternative reading that looks anything but a mistake, and therefore casts doubt on whether we are right to dismiss all the others as mistakes. In Pt IB for Χεβρων Zboc₂e₂ read Γαβαθα, and there seems to be no mistaking what place this is: consider by way of parallel the text and some variants at 1 Sam. 10: 26 Γαβαα] γαβαθα ca₂: γαβααθα A. The place in question is Saul's old capital city, Gibeah of Saul. And it makes excellent sense, of course, to say that Shimei came from Gibeah, for he was 'of the family of the house of Saul' (2 Sam. 16: 5), i.e. he was one of Saul's close relatives. Unfortunately we cannot know for certain whether the Lucianics' Γαβαθα is original and Χεβρων secondary, or whether Γαβαθα is a protest against an original Χεβρων. But it is interesting to see that the reading occurs also in Pt IA where the Γαβααθουρειμ of c_2 and the Γαβααθουρειν of b look like conflations of Γαβαα, or Γαβαθα, with Βαουρειμ (Bahurim). The Lucianics let neither Hebron nor Bahurim go unchallenged.

Now whether these readings entered the text early or late, it is evident that they are not mere scribal corruptions; they are deliberate entries that imply a good deal of thought. It is worth noting, therefore, that Shimei's ancestry and place of origin presented a problem which some later rabbis debated at length. In fact, it was one of three questions that brought R. Samuel bar Nahmani up from Babylon to the West in search of an answer.[18] The problem was this: in 2 Sam. 16: 5 and 19: 16 Shimei is described as 'of the family of the house of Saul' and 'from Bahurim'. Yet 2 Sam. 19: 20 says that when he came to meet David on David's return, he said: 'I am come down the first of all the house of Joseph to go down to meet my Lord the king.' How could Shimei, the rabbis asked, be both a member of the tribe of Benjamin and of the tribe of Joseph (i.e. Ephraim)? The solutions which the rabbis arrived at need not detain us here; but we cannot help wondering whether the Lucianics' reading of Χορραμ (2 Sam. 16: 5), Χορραν (19: 16 (17)) and Βαιθχορρων (17: 18) are not attempts to solve this problem by changing Bahurim into some city in Ephraim. Indeed it is very tempting to adopt Kittel's suggestion (BH³) that Βαιθχορρων represents בֵּית־חֹרֹן, Beth-horon, the well-known city in Ephraim's territory. On this showing the Lucianics' intention would be to say that, though a Benjamite, Shimei lived among the house of Joseph, and was the first from that territory to come down to meet the king. The snag is that בֵּית־חֹרֹן is normally transliterated Βαιθωρων (vel sim.), so that we cannot attach any certainty to the speculation.

Similarly the rabbis found another difficulty associated with Shimei.[19] A verse in Esther (2: 5) says that Mordecai was

descended from Shimei, the son of Kish, and was a Benjamite.
Yet the very same verse says that he was a Jew. The rabbis took
the term 'Jew' to mean 'of the tribe of Judah'; hence the
problem: how could Mordecai be both a Jew and a Benjamite?
They thought of many solutions. One of the less bizarre was
that offered by Rabbah b. Bar Ḥanah in the name of R. Joshua
b. Levi: 'His father was from Benjamin and his mother from
Judah.' Now this debate was, of course, about Mordecai, not
Shimei: but it may throw some light on the other peculiarity
in Pt IB, namely the doublet υἱὸς Γηρα υἱὸς σπέρματος τοῦ
Ιεμινι. Montgomery, as we have seen, thought that υἱὸς
σπέρματος was a clumsy mistake of the original translator which
was later glossed by the correct υἱὸς Γηρα. And so it may have
been; but theoretically it could also be that υἱὸς Γηρα was
original and υἱὸς σπέρματος a midrashic interpretation, which
for its purpose made use of the similar sound of גֵּרָא and זֶרַע.
Taken together with the other peculiarity of Pt IB, that Shimei
came from Hebron, this interpretation could be designed to
make the point that though Shimei geographically came from
Hebron, a city of Judah, physically he was of the seed of
Benjamin.

But this is only very uncertain speculation, and we had better
admit that we cannot anyway be sure whether Pt IB should be
regarded as part of Misc. 1 or part of the main Greek text. If
its peculiarities are clumsy errors, they could be a mark of the
original Greek; they could equally well be a reason for their
standing as incorrect and rejected readings in the miscellany.
If, on the other hand, they are of midrashic origin, it might
favour their being regarded as part of the miscellany; it could
not however rule out their being part of the main text. Indeed,
in a book so marked by layers of translation, revision, and re-
interpretation as 3 Reigns is, we are probably pushing analysis
too far in trying to decide this issue too closely.

CHAPTER 8

THE IMPLICATIONS

We must now attempt to sum up the results of our detailed analysis and to consider their implications. It can be said at once that there is no intention here of building some broad definitive theory of the history of the text on the slender basis of the evidence of the miscellanies. That would be absurd. On the other hand, the broad definitive theory, whenever (and if ever) it comes to be framed, will have to be able to account for the implications of the evidence of the miscellanies. For the simple fact is that they are an integral part of the textual evidence for 3 Reigns as we have it, and not some late and negligible addition to be found only in a few mediaeval manuscripts. Misc. 1 is present in every manuscript cited by BM, and the greater part of Misc. 2 in every one except the thorough-going hexaplaric witnesses, Ax Arm. Syr.

Let us begin, then, by reminding ourselves of those features of the miscellanies that make their evidence both unusual and significant. First, the miscellanies are collections of alternative translations, variant readings, glosses, doublets and the like. Now items of this sort are, of course, a very common textual feature in many manuscripts; but what is special about the miscellanies is that they have so large a number of such items all gathered together, and also that the items have been carefully edited and worked up into themes (see ch. 2).

Secondly, it is not uncommon in certain manuscripts to find incorporated into the text single variants and glosses, or even extensive passages, that are related in some way to the context into which they have been inserted. But again with the miscellanies it is different. Their component items have been taken from diverse contexts in differing parts of 3 Reigns, and, after being worked up into two themes, they have been inserted into the running narrative as paragraphs in their own right (see pp. 3–17).

Thirdly, all translation involves interpretation to some extent, and many instances of targumic paraphrase can be cited from all over the Greek Old Testament. But there is a difference in degree, and also sometimes in kind, between this type of interpretation and full-blown midrashic exegesis. And the two miscellanies not only contain individual examples of midrashic exegesis, but they are carefully arranged so that their very arrangement serves the purpose of making some midrashic point. They are the work not merely of a textual critic but of a Biblical expositor.

Moreover, we cannot dismiss the midrashic element in the miscellanies as an isolated phenomenon unconnected in character with the main Greek text. 3 Reigns has several examples of midrashic re-interpretation. In 18: 45; 20: 16, 25, 27 the peculiarities of the Greek (compared with the MT) show Ahab much more repentant and thus in a much better light than the MT does.[1] At 15: 5 the omission of the excepting clause in 'David did that which was right in the eyes of the Lord, and turned not aside from anything that he commanded him all the days of his life *save only in the matter of Uriah the Hittite*', is probably a deliberate attempt to defend his character.[2] The material of the Jeroboam story[3] has been re-arranged (see 11: 43, 12: 1–2) to give a substantially different interpretation of Jeroboam's part in the revolt; and at the same time an altogether different story of the revolt, having no counterpart in the MT, and radically conflicting with both it and the main Greek text, is given in 12: 24[a–z]. All the passages in 3 Reigns which deal with Solomon's activities in marrying Pharaoh's daughter, in amassing too much gold, and in acquiring too many horses – activities upon which the later rabbis frowned – all these passages (3: 1–2; 5: 14[a–b] [Ra; 4: 31–2 BM]; 9: 9[a] [Ra; 9: 9 end BM]; 9: 14, 26; 10: 22[a–c] [Ra; 10: 23–5 BM]) show signs of re-ordering and re-interpretation for the purpose of whitewashing Solomon.[4] Moreover, the concern over whether Solomon actually married Pharaoh's daughter or not, and if he did, exactly when, is shared, as we saw (pp. 66–73) both by the main Greek text and Misc. 1. In addition, the editor of

Misc. 1 goes out of his way by means of editorial comment to insist on the view that Solomon completed the temple before he built his own palace or any other buildings; and the main Greek text shows exactly the same concern: it changes the MT's order of the several parts of Solomon's building programme from temple, temple, palace, temple, to temple, temple, temple, palace.[5] The miscellanies, then, cannot be dismissed as mere appendages that have no significance for the main history of the text; they are clearly connected with some of its most important and prominent features.

Now in the last ten years our knowledge of the textual history of the four Books of Reigns in general has made extensive progress thanks largely to the epoch-making work of Barthélemy,[6] which revises Thackeray's earlier concepts and has itself been refined by F. M. Cross[7] and his pupil, Shenkel.[8] In the text-history, as they see it, we have these major stages: first, the Old Greek, to be equated in parts with the Lucianic text (Barthélemy) or followed by the proto-Lucianic text (Cross and Shenkel); then the 'kaige' recension, which in portions of the four Books sought to bring the Old Greek into line with the MT and to make it express certain minor grammatical and idiomatic features of the Hebrew that were exegetically important to the Palestinian rabbis who made this recension; then Origen's famous recension; then (but opinions differ) Lucian's recension proper, and perhaps other minor recensions. But when we ask where in this sequence of recensions does the editorial and midrashic activity fit which lies behind the existence, present form and position of the miscellanies, we find that there is no easy answer. That it was earlier than Origen's recension goes without saying;[9] but where it stands in relation to the 'kaige' recension is not directly apparent, since, according to Barthélemy and Shenkel,[10] the 'kaige' recension did not concern itself with 3 Reigns 2: 12 – 21: 43. There was, however, according to Barthélemy,[11] a second Palestinian recension (the 'kaige' recension was the first) which did concern itself with 3 Reigns 2: 12–21: 43; but he gives no examples of its readings in 3 Reigns. Shenkel, on the other hand, seems to deny[12] that this 'second Palestinian recension' was anything other than what is generally known as Theodotion. It thus appears that what is known about the general textual history of the four Books of Reigns offers little direct guidance in studying the problem of the miscellanies.

The only thing we can do in this connection, therefore, is to ask whether the miscellanies show any regular features similar to those of the recensions known in other parts of Reigns. And the answer provided by our analysis seems to be that though many individual instances can be found in the miscellanies that are similar to the features of one or other of the known recensions, the miscellanies as a whole show no one consistent or predominant tendency. And, as expected from Barthélemy's report, they show no features that are strictly peculiar to the 'kaige' recension.[13]

One major criterion by which recensions can be detected and characterised is their attitude to the MT. Both the 'kaige' and the Origenic recensions, for example, aim in different ways to bring their basic Greek text into closer conformity with the proto-MT or the MT itself. So let us sum up our findings in the miscellanies in this regard. First, the question of the MT's order. The miscellanies are aware of the order of the MT, for sometimes they are at pains to deny it, or at least to deny the inferences that might be drawn from the MT. This is apparent in the editorial comments about the order in which Solomon built the several parts of the temple and the royal palace (as we have just seen), and also in the editorial remarks on the timing of the building of Solomon's many cities (see pp. 8–9). On other occasions the miscellanies alter the MT's order of material, simply, it would seem, to make the material fit better into their schemes (see p. 11). On yet other occasions, however, the order of the material in the miscellanies is exactly that of the MT.

Secondly, the question of content. On many occasions the miscellanies have material that is in the MT but not in the main Greek text (see pp. 4, 40–3); but we also found clear indication that their motive was not systematically to supply that much of the MT which was missing in the main Greek text (see pp. 43, 52, 66). Sometimes they duplicated material that is both in the MT and in the main Greek text (see p. 34).

Thirdly, since the Qumran discoveries, we have become increasingly aware that the reason why the Greek translation differs from the Hebrew, and why the recensions of the Greek translation differ among themselves, is sometimes to be found in the use of Hebrew text traditions differing from the MT. And certainly we found examples of this in the miscellanies. But no consistent tendency! They will sometimes have a translation of the MT of 1 Kings while the main Greek text has a translation of a Hebrew text of Kings that differed from the MT of Kings and agreed with the MT of Chronicles (see pp. 67ff.). But they will on another occasion happily include two translations of one verse, one based on the MT and the other on a non-MT text (see pp. 43-4).

From this it appears that the miscellanies are not concerned to follow the MT or any other Hebrew text-tradition exclusively. In a sense they are not concerned with text as such; but rather, given textual variations, they attempt to make midrashic capital out of them.

A further criterion by which to distinguish recensions is whether they offer idiomatic or literalistic translation. Now compared with the main Greek text, the miscellanies on several occasions have the more idiomatic translation (see pp. 90-1, 99); yet on other occasions they have the more literalistic (see pp. 35, 91).

And even when it comes to midrashic interpretation and one makes the limited comparison of the miscellanies with the main Greek text, no consistency is to be found. In some instances the miscellanies have the same outlook and interpretation as the main Greek text (see pp. 107-8) and in others they have a different interpretation (see pp. 18, 70-3).

So then, the miscellanies show no consistent or predominant tendency; the only thing that unites their diverse component parts into two wholes is the two themes which they have been made to serve.

Next we must notice that the miscellanies seem not to be straight translations of a Hebrew text in which the component parts already stood together as they do now; rather the editing and compiling seem to have been done only after some at least of the individual pieces of material had already been translated into Greek. For the miscellanies, in spite of their themes and editorial comments, do not read as paragraphs of freely composed material; they are obviously collections of variants and doublets and such like. And some of these doublets are alternative translations of exactly the same Hebrew as lies behind the main Greek text (see pp. 34–7), and the sole point of their existence in the miscellanies seems to be simply that they offer an alternative *Greek* translation. On the other hand, if there is any truth in our analysis of v. f of Misc. 1 (see pp. 18ff.), in order to fit this material into the theme of the miscellany, the editor seems to have taken the MT, repointed and re-divided the words, and translated the result into Greek. And this would mean that the miscellanies were compiled in the light both of Hebrew texts and of Greek translations.

Now if we look around for some real-life situation from which 3 Reigns in its present form could have emanated, we shall obviously have to look further than a scriptorium where faithful scribes copied out as accurately as they could the Greek manuscript which lay before them. Similarly we shall have to go further than an individual scholar's study, or even 'a cell for two',[14] where in a comparatively short while a straightforward translation of the Hebrew *vorlage* was made. To account for the present state of the text seems to require something more like a rabbinic school, a Beth hamidrash, where varying Hebrew text-traditions and the comparative merits of alternative Greek renderings could be discussed; where opposite verdicts on the characters of the leading figures in the Book – David, Solomon, Jeroboam, Ahab – could be debated; and where in the light of the prevailing views the Greek translation could, where necessary, be worked over and revised; where apparent contradictions, such as those concerned with the number of Solomon's officers and servants (see pp. 50ff.) and of his horses (see p. 47) could have differing solutions applied to them; and where textual variants, both Hebrew and Greek, and alternative interpretations, which were not adjudged worthy to stand in the main body of the text, were still thought important enough to be the starting point of further midrash and worthy of being permanently recorded in the form of the miscellanies. Admittedly this means that 3 Reigns, whatever it was to start with, has developed a long way in the direction of being a midrash rather than a direct translation of a strictly Biblical text; but no other explanation seems to do justice to the facts.

Moreover the miscellanies' main feature of variant readings and alternative translations being made the starting point for further midrash bears striking resemblance to the phenomenon to which Prof. Talmon has called attention in his interesting study[15] 'Aspects of the textual transmission of the Bible in the light of Qumran manuscripts'. He points out (pp. 126ff.) that in the Babylonian Talmud there is a specific type of midrash in which an established text is suspended, as it were, and another reading, that is to say a textual variant, becomes the point of departure for an ensuing midrashic comment, by means of the introductory formula: 'do not read..., but rather read...' (the so-called '*al tiqrê* device). In the miscellanies we seem to have two midrashic themes built up in similar manner, the only, but important, differences being first that their starting point is not merely Hebrew textual variants, but alternative Greek translations and interpretations, and secondly that the midrash is built up largely of these elements and has the minimum of editorial comment and adaptation.

Now to say that 3 Reigns *in its present form* emanates from some rabbinic school is not the same thing as saying that the original translation was done in that school. The original translation was presumably done in Alexandria. Where was the revision done? We can give no definite answer, we can only speculate. If the items in the miscellanies had borne any distinctive marks of the 'kaige' recension, then we could have named Palestine as the source of the revision. Or if the main text, where it parallels the miscellanies, had regularly shown features that are strictly peculiar to the 'kaige' recension, we could have argued that the miscellanies were readings of the Old Greek, discarded when the 'kaige' recension inserted its revised readings into the main Greek text. But no such features appear. On the other hand, since 2 Reigns is marked so clearly with features of the Palestinian 'kaige' recension, it is reasonable to suppose that Palestine may have had a hand in the revision that brought 3 Reigns to its present form. Again, the literalistic exactitudes on which the 'kaige' recension insists find their *raison d'être* in a strict and rigorous halachic interpretation of the text. The midrashic, and often far-from-literalistic, interpretations of the miscellanies and of the main Greek text of 3 Reigns would fit more readily the spirit and methods of haggadah. But again, there is no reason why both kinds of interpretation should not have been performed on the Greek text in Palestine.

At the same time, if Alexandria contributed the original translation, we cannot be sure that Alexandria did not also contribute some of the re-interpretations. Actually, we are still remarkably ignorant on the question of who translated books like 3 Reigns. Aristeas never purported to tell us anything about the translation of books outside the Pentateuch and his story, as we all know, has to be largely discounted. Scholars conclude that the Greek Pentateuch was an 'authorised' translation made by the Jewish community in Alexandria and made primarily for that same community.[16] Suppose this was true of 3 Reigns likewise; yet what does it mean? What part of the community made it? Was it a production of the synagogue? or of an individual scholar appointed by the synagogue? or of a group of scholars, an early rabbinic school? And once the translation was made (whoever made it), was it regarded as beyond discussion and debate in the scholarly Jewish circles of Alexandria? Aristeas admittedly says[17] that once the Law was translated fearful curses were pronounced on any who should change it; but he protests too much. Biblical study, we know, was pursued with vigour in Alexandria by men like the Jewish scholar, Demetrius (*floruit*? 221–204 B.C.). His extant fragments[18] show him to have been not only interested in writing a history of the Jews down to his own times, but also engaged in answering people's questions[19] about difficulties and problems posed by the Biblical narrative. For example, by means of involved chronological and genealogical arguments he attempts to prove that the Ethiopian woman whom Moses married (Num. 12: 1) was not really an Ethiopian but a descendant of Abraham and Keturah.[20] One must admit, of course, that his arguments, though not sound, do attempt a more scholarly method than later midrash necessarily demanded; but the motive of defending the character of a prominent Biblical personality is not far removed from the motives that have led to the attempts to whitewash the characters of David, Solomon and even Ahab in 3 Reigns.

Furthermore, the fact that Demetrius shows such great interest in chronology[21] in general, and also uses chronology to explain away what he felt was a problem, cannot but remind us that one of the outstanding peculiarities of 3 Reigns is that for certain parts of the history it has two conflicting systems of chronology, which have produced duplicate and different translations of certain sizeable passages. One set of duplicates agrees with the MT in its chronology and, consequently, in its narrative order, while in small details of language it is consistently conformed to the MT. The other set has a different chronology and narrative order and is not conformed to the MT in the details of its language. Shenkel, who has recently made a special study of this problem,[22] may well be right in maintaining that the set of duplicates that follows the MT was added by the Palestinian 'kaige' recension, and that the set that disagrees with the MT represents the Old Greek translation. But that would not exclude the possibility that the Old Greek itself was already a re-interpretation by learned Alexandrians like Demetrius, concerned to explain away the notorious, apparent difficulties of the MT's chronology. [22a]

In this connection of possible Alexandrian contributions to the re-interpretations to be found in 3 Reigns, we might also recall the marked interest in the temple's water supply evinced by Misc. 1 (see pp. 30–3). Admittedly this is a small and uncertain piece of evidence; but an interest which weaves together details into an unrealistic account out of admiration for the wonder of the temple's water supply is perhaps more typical of Alexandrians like Aristeas, than 1st century A.D. Palestinians to whom the facts of the temple's water system were common knowledge.

But when all is said, the only certainty which we can claim is that the miscellanies and 3 Reigns as they now stand bear many marks of the studies and debates of a rabbinic school, or schools, in Palestine or Alexandria or both.

Finally, the fact that both the miscellanies and the main text of 3 Reigns contain midrashic interpretation, some of which is fanciful in the extreme, raises the question of the early Jewish and the Christian attitude to the authority of the Septuagint. Judging from what we actually know of this same phenomenon in later times, it seems quite clear that it does not mean that the early Jews had no clear distinction in their minds between Bible and interpretation. As the centuries went by, midrash grew ever more free and fanciful. The liberties it allowed itself of repointing, re-division of words, play on words and so forth, in the exposition even of the Hebrew are almost beyond our modern understanding. But far from this implying that for the later rabbis the distinction between Bible and interpretation was very blurred, we know that they had the clearest possible conception of the distinction between midrash and Bible. And therefore we have no reason to think that the milder forms of midrash practised by the early rabbis on the Greek translation meant that they made no distinction between the Hebrew Biblical text on the one hand and midrashim, Greek or Hebrew, on the other. And for Alexandria, at least, we may go further, and say that when Demetrius' Gentile contemporaries were constantly at work in the great library on the textual criticism of classical authors, it is difficult to think that Demetrius, for all his great learning, had no concept of what textual criticism was, or of Biblical 'text' in the narrowest, technical sense.[23] In interpretation he and his colleagues might well allow themselves what appear to us great liberties; and translation for them was very heavily concerned with interpretation. But this is certainly not evidence that they failed to see any distinction between Bible and interpretation, between an authoritative Hebrew original and a disputable Greek translation. And as for the Palestinian Jews, the fact that they constantly thought it worthwhile by their revisions to make the Greek translation conform ever more closely to the Hebrew texts shows clearly enough where they thought authority lay.

At this point someone may well protest that the Alexandrian Jew, Philo, regarded the Greek translation of the Pentateuch as inspired. Certainly he says[24] of the translators: '...they became as it were possessed, and, under inspiration, wrote, not each several scribe something different, but the same word for word, as though dictated to each by an invisible prompter.' But if one puts this account side by side with that of Aristeas, one finds that the earlier Alexandrian had a much more realistic idea of the process of translating: the translators made 'all details harmonise by mutual comparisons'.[25] No miracle of inspiration here! The only near-miracle Aristeas will claim is that the seventy-two translators completed the work 'in seventy-two days, as if this coincidence had been the result of some design'.[26] Josephus, moreover, who lived just after Philo, gives a similarly realistic account of the translation: the translators 'set to work as ambitiously and painstakingly as possible to make the translation accurate' (*Antiquities*, XII, 104). Philo's exaggerated and somewhat superstitious view of the accuracy and authority of the Greek translation cannot be held to be representative of Judaism, not even of Alexandrian Judaism.

In Christendom the Septuagint, used as a convenient translation by the early missionaries to Greek-speaking parts, came eventually to be more and more highly regarded until it was accepted virtually as 'The Bible', equally authoritative as the Hebrew original. In consequence, when Jerome exposed its inadequacies, mistakes, unauthorised interpretations and additions by producing an Old Testament translated direct from the Hebrew, people like Augustine were understandably upset.[27]

But as with Philo in Judaism (whose exaggerations some of the Church Fathers followed), so with the Christian Fathers: excessive veneration of the Greek translation was a development of later, post-Apostolic, times. The New Testament shows a more realistic attitude: it uses the Septuagint widely and takes over some of its interpretations. But it does not confine itself to the Septuagint, as though the Septuagint were a uniquely authoritative translation, to be used on all occasions invariably and unquestioningly. When they so prefer, New Testament writers use other translations. Their use of some parts of the many and varied Greek translations that go under the name of Septuagint cannot fairly be held to indicate that they would have accepted, as inspired, strange and fanciful interpretations such as those that we have found in the miscellanies and main Greek text of 3 Reigns.

NOTES TO THE TEXT

1 *The Old Testament in Greek*, II, Part II, ed. by A. E. Brooke, N. McLean and H. St J. Thackeray (Cambridge, 1930). Hereafter the abbreviation BM will be used to denote this volume, and, where appropriate, any other volume of this edition of the Greek OT.

2 *Septuaginta id est Vetus Testamentum Graece iuxta LXX interpretes*, edidit A. Rahlfs (Stuttgart, 1935).

3 BM and Rahlfs differ over the division of the material between v. 35^e and v. 35^f. I shall be following Rahlfs' division.

4 Indeed that is how Hänel described it (*ZAW* 47 [1929], 76–9): 'die Zusätze wirklich nichts anderes als eine Varientensammlung sein wollen'.

5 Basically, but not necessarily in all details; and in cases like this sometimes, though not always, the differences in translation are caused by differences in the Hebrew *vorlage*.

6 See the remarks by Montgomery on this score in his article 'The supplement at the end of 3 Kingdoms 2 (I Reg. 2)', *ZAW* 50 (1932), 124–9, and in the appropriate sections of his *ICC Kings* (Edinburgh: T. and T. Clark, 1951).

1 *JSS* 13 (1968), 76–92.

2 *Textus* VII (1969), 1–29.

3 The uncertainty arises because the MT of 6: 38^b simply says 'and he was building it seven years' whereas our v. c says ἐν ἑπτὰ ἔτεσιν ἐποίησεν καὶ συνετέλεσεν. The indication that in spite of the differences the two verses are counterparts is as follows. The MT of 6: 37 and 38 says 'In the fourth year was the foundation of the house of the Lord laid, in the month Ziv. And in the eleventh year, in the month Bul, which is the eighth month, was the house finished throughout all the parts thereof, and according to all the fashion of it. And he was building it seven years.' Now the main Greek text has a clear and undisputed counterpart of all this *except the last sentence*, though it stations it in a different place, at 6: 1$^{c \text{ and } d}$ (Rahlfs; BM 6: 4 and 5). But of the last sentence the Greek has nowhere a counterpart unless our v. c^β is the counterpart. If, how-

ever, the differences between v. c and the MT 6: 38^b are too great for these verses to be regarded as counterparts, the fact that v. c$^\beta$ would then have no known Hebrew behind it (though it could be based on a non-MT-type Hebrew text) would raise the possibility that it is an editor's adaptation or invention. But in any case the main point – that v. c is made up of material taken from two different contexts – remains unaffected.

4 For a full discussion of this editorial concern and its relation to the ordering of the main Greek text and to the contentions of later midrashim, see *JSS* 13 (1968), 90–1.

5 See note 3 above.

6 See p. 6 above.

7 For a comparison between the miscellany and the main Greek text see *Textus* VII (1969), 6–7.

8 See above, p. 7.

9 See, for example, 1 Kings 14: 21; 15: 1, 33; 16: 8.

10 See J. D. Shenkel, *Chronology and recensional development in the Greek text of Kings* (Cambridge, Mass., 1968), pp. 51f.

11 *ICC Kings*, pp. 206–9.

12 Whatever those activities were. The translation adopted here, for the sake of argument, 'began to breach (or capture) the fortresses of the Lebanon', is the one suggested by Montgomery, *JAOS* (1936), p. 137.

NOTES TO CHAPTER 3 (pages 18–29)

1 The reason for this will become apparent in a moment.

2 There is something like it at 9: 9 (end) which has no known Hebrew authority for standing there. It is discussed below in another connection, p. 69.

3 See *ZAW* 50 (1932), 127.

4 It is possible, as Montgomery admits, that מסגרת was treated as a plural, which would then support the mss which read ἐπάλξεις. But for the rest, since no later scribe intent on bringing the Greek text nearer to the Hebrew would have been as likely to divide and point his Hebrew in this extraordinary fashion as would the original translator, the readings which stand closest to the Hebrew as demanded by this singular interpretation, are most likely to be original. Other readings, which present elements not in the Hebrew, are likely to be additions made later, regardless of the Hebrew, to help out the sense. Thus there should be no καὶ τὰς before ἔπαλξιν (-εις) and no καὶ before διέκοψεν. This latter point is particularly important. See also Montgomery's discussion in his note to the article in *ZAW* 50 (1932), 127, cited above.

5 The significance of this is discussed below, pp. 67ff., 130 n. 22a.

6 Taken from the Babylonian Talmud, *Sanhedrin* 101a, translated by H. Freedman (Soncino edition, 1935).

7 See, for example, Babylonian Talmud, *Berakoth* 21b (translation by Maurice Simon [Soncino edition, 1948]): 'And should you say that R. Judah does not derive lessons from the juxtaposition of texts, (this does not matter) since R. Joseph has said: Even those who do not derive lessons from the juxtaposition of texts in all the rest of the Torah, do so in Deuteronomy...' See also, for juxtaposition, Midrash Rabbah, *Leviticus* xxv, 8.

8 Midrash Rabbah, *Numbers* xix, 16, translated by J. J. Slotki (Soncino Press edition, 1951, p. 765).

9 See for instance the extravagant lengths to which the Jerusalem Talmud (*Sanhedrin* x, 2) is prepared to go in inventing a long story to explain the connection between the verse 'And Elijah the Tishbite,...said unto Ahab, As the Lord...lives...there shall not be dew nor rain these years...' (1 Kings 17: 1) and the verse which precedes it, 'In his days did Hiel...build Jericho...with the loss of Abiram his firstborn, and... with the loss of his youngest son Segub...according to the word of the Lord...by Joshua...' (1 Kings 16: 34).

10 For a random example see Midrash Rabbah, *Leviticus* xvii, 3: '[We know that leprosy comes] for robbing the public, from [the experience of] Shebna...Whence [do we know] that he was stricken with leprosy? – Since it is said, *Behold, the Lord...will wrap thee round and round* (Isa. xxii, 17); "*Wrap thee round*" must refer to a leper, of whom it is said, *And he shall wrap himself over the upper lip* (Lev. xiii, 45)' (translation by J. Israelstam).

11 For random examples see *The Midrash on Psalms*, 9: 1 '*also He hath set ha'olam (the world) in their heart (bĕlibbam)* (Eccles. 3: 11). R. Berechiah said in the name of R. Jonathan: do not read *ha'olam*, "the world", but *ha'olĕlim*, "the little children"; the verse means therefore that God has set love of little children in their fathers' hearts' (translation by W. G. Braude). See also *ibid.* 9: 17, where in the verse, 'Therefore do the maidens love thee', עֲלָמוֹת is broken up and repointed עַל מוּת, and the verse is then interpreted to mean 'Therefore do they love Thee unto death.'

12 For the various interpretations of *Millo* in the meaning 'filling', see K. Kenyon, *Jerusalem* (Thames and Hudson, London, 1967), p. 50.

13 Translation by M. Simon (Soncino Press, London, 1951).

14 It is true that only Bboa₂c₂e₂ Eth. lack the limitation; the majority add ἀπὸ τοῦ ποταμοῦ γῆς Φυλιστιαιῶν καὶ ἕως ὁρίου Αἰγύπτου. But as Rahlfs has pointed out (*Septuaginta-Studien*, 3 Heft [1911], p. 212) the inflected form Φυλιστίαῖοι (as against ἀλλόφυλοι or Φυλιστιειμ) is uncharacteristic of the original LXX, and betrays the whole phrase as a later addition.

15 In the passage from *Song of Songs* I. I. 10 quoted above, p. 23.

16 It differs from the MT in one or two small details. The significance of the details is discussed below, pp. 43ff.

17 The main Greek text at 5: 4 (Rahlfs; BM 4: 24) has a counterpart of MT 5: 4, but it omits the phrase in question. When Origen supplied the missing phrase he put ἀπὸ Θαψα ἕως Γάζης. His Θαψα, as one might expect, is tolerably near to the Hebrew.

18 *ZAW* 50 (1932), 128–9.

NOTES TO CHAPTER 4 (pages 30–49)

1 It is true that the term τὰ ὑποστηρίγματα is also used in 3 Reigns 10: 12 of 'supports' or 'props' for the temple and royal palace; but since all the other items in v. e are from the temple court, and τὰ ὑποστηρίγματα follow the 'sea' and precede the 'lavers', it is reasonable to assume that they here refer to the 'supports' of the 'sea', 7: 11 (MT 7: 24). Actually ὑποστηρίγματα mistranslates the Hebrew which has פְּקָעִים 'gourds'.

2 These are more frequently called χυτρόκαυλος (7: 24, 29); but the term λουτήρ is also used (7: 17).

3 *Aristeas to Philocrates*, edited and translated by M. Hadas (New York, 1951), p. 135.

4 The word he uses, πηγή, occurs in ms 246 in our v. e thus τὴν κρήνην πηγῆς.

5 ἐλατομήθη is a conjectural emendation of the mss' impossible ἠλαττώθη. See Rahlfs.

6 See the discussion in *JSS* 13 (1968), 85.

7 All mss except Bha₂ have some noun like σοφία between ἐπληθύνθη and Σαλωμων, which brings the Greek nearer to the MT. Syr. has *sapientia* sub ·※· γ'. It is possible that an original ἡ φρόνησις was at some stage accidentally omitted, and later the gap was filled in with σοφία from the Hexapla. Or, perhaps, the omission is original. But the difference is of no great significance.

8 Translated by A. Cohen (Soncino Press, London, 1951).

9 For this reading see ch. 3, n. 4 above.

10 In the hexaplaric text at 9: 15, presented by Ax Arm. Syr., we have σὺν τὴν μελω καὶ τὴν ἄκραν τοῦ περιφράξαι τὸν φραγμὸν τῆς πόλεως Δαυιδ... Now σὺν τὴν μελω is obviously a doublet of τὴν ἄκραν, both representing אֶת־הַמִּלּוֹא. The rendering of אֶת by σὺν is Aquilanic, but the fact that one then gets the doublet καὶ τὴν ἄκραν, and that there is nothing in the MT to correspond to the phrase τοῦ περιφράξαι... Δαυιδ, suggests that what we have in Ax Arm. Syr. is not pure Aquila but the original LXX plus hexaplaric addition. In which case τοῦ περιφράξαι

compared with συνέκλεισεν is but a stylistic variant emanating from the original translator.

11 I once suggested (*VT* 15 [1965], 335; in that article I used the verse-numbering of BM which differs from Rahlfs') that 2: 35$^{f\alpha}$ was the older translation, which was ousted from its place when the newer and more correct translation, 10: 22^a, took its place. I do not think so now. V. f$^\alpha$ is, after all, an alternative not to 10: 22^a but to 11: 27. Moreover, at the time I was impressed by Montgomery's dictum that crude mistranslations are a mark of the Old Greek. But if I am right in my suspicion that v. f$^\alpha$ is not a crude mistake but a midrashic re-interpretation, then it follows that midrashic re-interpretations are not likely to be the original translation but a later addition, thought up in the schools by further study of both original text and early translation.

12 Bjna$_2$ read ἀνοίγειν.

13 The Greek names are given as restored in spelling by Rahlfs.

14 Ḳrê, תַּדְמֹר.

15 *ZAW* 50 (1932), 128–9.

16 *JAOS* (1936), p. 137.

17 Since τοῦ δυναστεῦσαι αὐτοὺς in 1 Chron. 16: 21 represents לְעָשְׁקָם, it is possible that τὰ δυναστεύματα goes back to some form of the root חשק, deliberately re-interpreted as עשק, in the phrase וְאֵת חֵשֶׁק שְׁלֹמֹה אֲשֶׁר חָשַׁק לִבְנוֹת...בַּלְּבָנוֹן.

18 The verse numbering is that of Rahlfs which throughout this context differs from that of BM.

19 It was added later by Origen and is present in Ax Arm. Syr.

20 We have already seen (p. 26) how significant this last omission is.

21 The reading ὁρίων is that of the majority: boc$_2$e$_2$ however read ὁρίου.

22 The reading ὁρίων is that of B N Arm.; the majority have ὁρίου.

23 *VT* 19 (1969), 454–63. In this article I used BM's verse numbering.

24 The translation τοκάδες ἵπποι, *brood mares*, where the Hebrew has אֻרוֹת סוּסִים *stalls of horses*, is a striking difference of meaning, but it can be accounted for without postulating a Hebrew *vorlage* different from the MT; see J. Gray, *I and II Kings*, 1st edit. (S.C.M. Press, London, 1964), p. 245 n. e.

25 Rahlfs' verse numbering; in BM it is 10: 29.

26 See the later rabbinic discussion (Babylonian Talmud, *Sanhedrin* 21b) of these discordant numbers.

27 Note the additional argument for the misplacing of this 'correction' in the *VT* article referred to above, n. 23.

NOTES TO CHAPTER 5 (pages 50–92)

1 We have already seen (p. 11) what is the reason for this change of order.

2 Rahlfs' verse-numbering (BM's equivalent of 10: 22a–c is 10: 23–5; of 4: 14b is 4: 32).

3 *VT* 15 (1965), 325–35.

4 Only the mss B*b′ omit the noun ἐργοδιώκτας.

5 A mixture of Ķrê הַנִּצָּבִים and Kethîb הַנְּצִיבִים.

6 The Greek has no equivalent of בעם; only the mss AZbxc₂e₂ Arm. Syr. (sub ·※·) have τοῦ λαοῦ. But it is interesting to see that bc₂e₂ Eth. (vid.) have (τοῦ λαοῦ) τῶν ποιούντων τὰ ἔργα, which makes the ἐπιστάται to be *not* working foremen, but officers over the workers. This is the same interpretation which appears in v. h of Misc. 1.

7 Montgomery, *ICC Kings*, p. 137, would explain the figure 3,300 as follows. Originally, the Hebrew text knew only of a levy raised from all Israel of 30,000 men (1 Kings 5: 27). Then following the 'later invention' of the enslavement of the Canaanites according to MT 1 Kings 9: 20–2 and 2 Chronicles 8: 8–10, 150,000 Canaanites (70,000 bearers and 80,000 hewers) were interpolated into the MT of 1 Kings 5: 29. Then some arithmetically minded editor got to work. In his mind he added together the 30,000 Israelites and the 150,000 Canaanites, to get a total of 180,000 workers. Then he asked himself what number of superintendents would be necessary for a force of 180,000 workers. Casting around he found the number 550 applied to superintendents in 1 Kings 9: 23 (which passage Montgomery assumes is original, though 9: 20–2 he regards as a later invention). The editor then realised, we must presume, that the figure 550 was original and was the number of superintendents over the 'original' 30,000 *Israelite* workers. But now, having added the 'interpolated' 150,000 Canaanites to the original 30,000 Israelites, he felt he must himself interpolate a force of superintendents for the new total in strict proportion to the number of superintendents for the old total. So he set himself the problem: what value of x will satisfy the equation $550:30{,}000 = x:180{,}000$? The answer was, of course, 3,300. Montgomery felt that this was a 'nice piece of editorial arithmetic'. I find it, I must say, incredible. And as for the Chronicler's story about the enslavement of the Canaanites being an invention: the use of Canaanites as forced labourers to hew wood and draw water was surely not first thought up by Solomon, let alone the Chronicler. And if Solomon's ambitious building programmes demanded a levy of 30,000 Israelites, as MT 1 Kings 5: 27 says, is it likely that he would *not* have used Canaanites as well, and more of them than of Israelites?

8 Most mss have τρεῖς, but this is an itacism; read τρίς with gh Arm. Syr. = MT שָׁלֹשׁ פְּעָמִים.

9 Though already we have seen (p. 9) that the positioning of the MT's equivalent of the last part of the verse, καὶ συνετέλεσεν τὸν οἶκον, in relation to the rest of the paragraph in the MT, probably led to the editorial protest registered in v. k of Misc. 1, and perhaps helps to account for the presence of v. g itself in the miscellany as a 'rejected reading'.

10 See John Gray, *I and II Kings*, 1st ed. (S.C.M. Press, London, 1964), pp. 235–6.

11 Whereas the hexaplaric mss attempt a rendering with αὐτός.

12 Ba₂ omit τὸν οἶκον αὐτοῦ καὶ.

13 Omitted by Ba₂.

14 Babylonian Talmud, *Yebamoth* 76a–b, translated by I. W. Slotki (Soncino Press, 1936).

15 Emphasis on *love*, *sc.* he did not *marry* them.

16 Its existence, or something like it, in the mss bgoc₂e₂ seems a late addition.

17 Unfortunately what that 'all' was is rendered somewhat uncertain by the variant: τὸν οἶκον κυρίου Ba₂] pr. αυτου τον οικον και boc₂e₂: τον οικον αυτου και τον οικον κυριου AMN rell. Eth. Syr. The fact that B frequently indulges in omissions would incline one to think that the longer reading is original; and Rahlfs so decides. But the decision is complicated by the fact that the editor has himself added the information that 'in *seven* years he made and finished'. Seven years is the time it took to build the house of the Lord, and does not, according to the main text, include the completion of the king's house which took thirteen years. On the other hand, if Pharaoh's daughter came up out of David's city immediately upon completion of the Lord's house, before Solomon's palace was built, she would have had no house to go to, for obviously, the house she went to was the house mentioned in 7: 45b (MT 7: 8) which was built as part of the palace complex. Of course the editor of the miscellany may have had his own version of the building timetable differing from that of the main text; but it is evident that both the miscellany and the main text are moving at the secondary level of attempted exegesis, rather than at the primary level of simple text-transmission. And at this level the editor of the miscellany would not have hesitated to omit the phrase 'and his own house', if that omission was necessary to support his scheme of interpretation.

18 Translated by J. J. Slotki (Soncino Press), p. 351.

19 Translated by J. Israelstam (Soncino Press), p. 158.

20 The words in brackets occur in all the mss except Ba₂. Rahlfs thinks them secondary and maybe he is right; but B and its close follower a₂ are notorious for their unintentional omissions.

21 The main Greek text has no counterpart of either MT 4: 20 or MT 5: 5; see pp. 41–2.

22 Translated by H. Freedman (Soncino Press, 1935).

23 Dr Freedman explains: 'Cooks used to place dough above the pot, to absorb the steam and vapour.'

24 The provisions listed would obviously not have been enough for all Israel and Judah; but apart from that, this explanation would tend in the opposite direction to the exaggerations of the earlier explanations. Midrash, however, is not shy of such inconsistencies in the various explanations it offers.

25 For a full discussion see T. N. D. Mettinger, *Solomonic State Officials*, Coniectanea Biblica, O.T. Series 5 (Gleerup, Lund, 1971), especially pp. 134–9.

26 Rahlfs reads πατριᾶς; but this seems to be a corruption for στρατιᾶς: see his *Septuaginta-Studien* III (1911), 201. See also p. 82 above.

27 Such as the lists of David's princes given in 2 Sam. 9: 15–18, 20: 23–6; 1 Chron. 27: 32–4.

28 For a full discussion see Montgomery, *ICC Kings* (1951), pp. 112–119; K. A. Kitchen, *Theological Students' Fellowship Bulletin*, No. 41 (1965), 17; M. Noth, *Biblischer Kommentar* (Könige, 1965), IX, 1, 55–9.

29 = Main Greek text.

30 Zbnxya₂c₂e₂ read αὐτῷ – this is even nearer to the MT.

31 But see the note to Rahlfs' text.

32 In 2 Sam. 8: 18 the remark 'And David's sons were priests' is translated υἱοὶ Δαυιδ αὐλάρχαι ἦσαν – court-officials – an intelligent translation of כהן used in a non-religious sense. On the other hand in 2 Sam. 20: 26, where for the MT's 'And Ira also the Jairite was priest unto David' most Greek mss have καὶ γε Ειραι ὁ Ιαρειν ἦν ἱερεὺς τοῦ Δαυιδ, the Lucianics, boc₂e₂ Thdt, have substituted the name of a well-known priest, Jehoiada: καὶ Ιωδαε (vel sim.) ὁ Ιεθερ ἦν ἱερεὺς τῷ Δαυιδ.

33 For a discussion of these names see J. A. Montgomery, *ICC Kings*, pp. 113–17 and K. A. Kitchen, *T.S.F. Bulletin*, 41 (1965), 17.

34 Main text: Σαβα Ba₂] σιβα efmw: *Suba* Eth.: σαφατ Zboc₂e₂: σαφατι b′: *Susa* La.: σισαν v: σειρα y: ισα x: εισαι i: σεισα AMN rell. Arm. Misc. 2: Σουβα] σαβα e: σουσα Z (vid.) boc₂e₂ dgp La.

35 The only other variants are σαβα h; σουβα a₂; σασαβα 242; all of which seem to be confusions with the σουβα/σαβα/σουσα of Item 2.

36 According to the margins of jz at 2 Reigns 8: 16 ἀναμιμνήσκων is the term preferred by Aquila.

37 D. Barthélemy, *Les Devanciers d'Aquila* (Leiden, 1963), p. xi *et passim*.

38 The full evidence as given by Brooke–McLean is: for the main Greek text: καὶ] pr. ÷ Syr.: om. bdp | ιωσαφαθ B] *Iosafet* Eth.: ιωσασαφατ b: ιωσαφ z: ιωσαφατ AMNZ (vid.) b′ rell. Arm. La. | αχειλιαδ Ba₂] αχιληδ ef: αχιλουδ hj: αχιλαδ N: αχιλιθ x: αχελλειδ i: αχιθαλαμ Z (vid.) o: αχειθαλααμ c₂: αχιταλαμ be₂: αχιλιδ M rell. Arm.: αχιμα A:

Achiad Eth.: *Achia* La. | ὑπομιμνήσκων BZ (vid.) boc₂e₂ a₂] αναμιμνη-
σκων AMN rell.: *a memoria* La.

for Misc. 2: βασα] σαβα h: σουβα a₂: ⟨σασαβα 242⟩: βαρακ Z (vid.)
bdgopc₂e₂ La. | αχειθαλαμ] εχιθαλαμ gc₂: αχειταλαμ e₂: αχιλαθαμ f:
αχιθαλα h: ⟨αχιθαμαν 236⟩: *Acastobi* La. | ἀναμιμνήσκων] αναμιμνησκω
i*: *memoria* La.

39 στρατεια is but an itacism for στρατιά (army); it is not to be understood as a deliberate vocabulary variant, στρατεία (expedition).

40 Ιωαδ is their consistent translation of Jehoiada throughout the Books of
Reigns.

41 See A. Rahlfs, *Septuaginta-Studien*, III, 201.

42 This is Rahlfs' reconstructed text; the A and B traditions are much
different.

43 See J. C. Greenfield, 'Cherethites and Pelethites', *Interpreter's Dictionary
of the Bible* (Abingdon Press, New York, 1962), I, 557.

44 Unless by chance the variant Ιωαδ (the Lucianic form for Jehoiada),
offered in Misc. 2 by b, is not a corruption of the majority reading Ιωαβ,
but the survival of an original (Βαναιας υἱός) Ιωαδ (Ιωδαε), which the
rest have corrupted into Ιωαβ.

45 But contrast the punctuation of the Jerusalem Bible: 'Benaiah son of
Jehoiada, the chief priest'.

46 So Montgomery, *ICC Kings*, p. 115 and the RV margin 'Or *chief
minister*'.

47 b has τῶν ἱερέων; c₂ has an obvious corruption, τῶν ὀρέων.

48 The translations given below are those or I. Epstein, in the Soncino
edition of the Babylonian Talmud (London, 1935).

49 This verse is meant to be a quotation of 1 Chron. 27: 34. Epstein has
this explanatory note: 'The Biblical version of the verse is *Jehoiada the
son of Benaiah*. Tosaf. Ḥananel and Aruk (art. אחר a.) base their versions
on this reading and comment accordingly. Rashi and this translation
follow the text of the printed editions of the Talmud which agree with
II Sam. XX, 23 and 1 Chron. XVIII, 17.'

60 This exegesis is obtained by interpreting כְּרֵתִי as though it were a word
formed from כָּרַת 'to cut'. It has, of course, nothing to do with כָּרֵת.

51 As though פְּלֵתִי were from פלא 'wonder'; it isn't, of course.

52 'I.e., only after the Sanhedrin had authorised a war was there any
need for Joab, the chief general.' – Epstein. This interpretation, it is
interesting to notice, is arrived at by assuming that the very order of
the names in this list of David's officers is significant.

53 See, e.g., Bab. Talmud, *Berakoth* 4a; Midrash on the Psalms, 3, 3.

54 See L. Ginzberg, *Legends of the Jews* (Philadelphia, 5th impression, 1968),
VI, 302.

55 See footnote 32 and p. 86.

56 In this case the πλινθείου of Misc. 2 may well be an itacism for πλινθίου.

57 Montgomery (*ICC Kings*, pp. 113–18) thought that both ἐπὶ τῆς αὐλαρχίας and ἐπὶ τοῦ πλινθ(ε)ίου were misplaced glosses, that πλινθίον meant 'quadrans' (an instrument for determining the seasons by the length of the sun's shadow), that ἐπὶ τοῦ πλινθίου was the title of an officer who was responsible for the official calendar, and that under Solomon this officer was Azariah b. Sadok. This theory involved Montgomery in the necessity of explaining the reading of the Lucianics in 2 Sam. 20: 23 as 'a rash application by the later Theodotion of material he obtained from (1 Kings) 2: 46^h' (i.e. from Misc. 2). Certainly the margin of j at 2 Sam. 20: 23 attributes the Lucianics' reading to θ', and possibly rightly so; but Montgomery's main theory, though ingenious, is not convincing (for a criticism of it see K. A. Kitchen, *The Theological Students' Fellowship Bulletin* 41 [1965], 17), and it is unlikely that Theodotion or the Lucianics of 2 Sam. 20: 23 were dependent on Misc. 2.

58 AM (text) N and the majority of the minuscules read Αζαριας, but they are probably under hexaplaric influence.

59 B and A, with some supporters add καὶ Ελιακ ὁ οἰκονόμος – an apparent doublet which the majority do not have.

60 In no other item is the verb 'to be' used.

61 The Lucianics have Αχικαμ.

62 The Lucianics have θαρακ, the Old Latin *Aza*.

63 The Lucianics have Εδραμ; cf. the name of the officer in Item 9 as given by Misc. 2, and also the reading Ιεζεδραν for Αδωνιραμ presented by the Lucianics in 2 Sam. 20: 24.

64 In 3 Reigns 10: 22a (= MT 1 Kings 9: 15) προνομή is used, though v. 22b reverts to φόρος.

NOTES TO CHAPTER 6 (pages 93–5)

1 There is no other similar phrase in the OT.

2 The MT has an equivalent verse at 5: 4.

3 The difference in tense οὐκ ἔστιν/οὐκ ἦν is occasioned by the fact that in 5: 18 οὐκ ἔστιν occurs in a letter written from Solomon to Hiram, in which the present tense is the only one possible. In Misc. 2 the context requires a past tense. So the difference has nothing to do with the feature called by Barthélemy 'Intemporalité de la negation d'existence' (*Les Devanciers*, p. 65).

4 But not this time including the Lucianics boc₂e₂.

1 I have discussed this point in detail in 'The Shimei Duplicate and its Satellite Miscellanies', *JSS* 13 (1968), 76–92, and further demonstrated its connection with the peculiar order of contents of 3 Reigns in 'Problems of Text and Midrash in the Third Book of Reigns', *Textus* VII (1969), 1–29.

2 'Now therefore hold him not guiltless, for thou art a wise man; and thou wilt know what thou oughtest to do unto him…'

3 See 'The Supplement at End of 3 Kingdoms 2', *ZAW* 50 (1932), 124–9.

4 See *Chronology and Recensional Development in the Greek Text of Kings* (Cambridge, Massachusetts, 1968), p. 114.

5 *Les Devanciers*, pp. 78–80.

6 AMN bgijnopvxyc$_2$e$_2$ read ἀπάντησιν.

7 Notably boc$_2$e$_2$.

8 'The Greek Translators of the Four Books of Kings', *JTS* 8 (1907), 262–78.

9 And he also suggested yet another book division, 'The Supplement', *ZAW* 50 (1932), 124ff.

10 *Septuaginta-Studien* III, 186ff.

11 Against this theory one might argue that if it were true, the execution of Joab, 3 Reigns 2: 28–35, ought to be preceded by a duplicate account of David's dying charge to Solomon to execute him, 3 Reigns 2: 5–6 (it falls in the Lucianics' 2 Reigns). But actually 2: 12–28 gives a sufficient explanation for his execution: he had joined the attempt of Adonijah on the throne, and therefore when Adonijah was executed for another indirect attempt (12–27) Joab took fright and sought sanctuary – thus giving evidence of his sense of guilt.

12 For a full account of this recension see Barthélemy, *Les Devanciers*.

13 The recension is said by Barthélemy to have covered 2 Sam. 11: 2 – 1 Kings 2: 11, by Shenkel (*Chronology and Recensional Development*, pp. 117ff.), 2 Sam. 10: 1 – 1 Kings 2: 11.

14 Montgomery ('The Supplement', *ZAW* 50 [1932], 124ff.) thought that a definite answer could be given: 'In examination of this supplementary material we must note that the whole extent of 𝔊 2: 35^a–46^l is to be included from the standpoint of the make-up of the Greek book; that is, the Shimei episode in its two acts, v. 35$^{l–o}$ and vv. 36–46, although wholly agreeing with 𝔖, except in the combination of the acts, is equally supplementary with the other material. We have therefore to block out three groups in this supplement: the first miscellany, the Shimei story, the second miscellany. And we doubtless have to assume that the additions were built up on this order.'

15 'The Supplement', pp. 124ff.

16 Exactly where was Bahurim? S. R. Driver, *Notes on the Hebrew Text and Topography of the Books of Samuel*, 2nd edit. (Oxford, 1912), p. 248, says E.N.E. of Jerusalem; Y. Aharoni and M. Avi-Yonah, *The Macmillan Bible Atlas* (NewYork/London, 1968), p. 71 (map 109), show it almost due south of Jerusalem. Was it, then, in the territory of Benjamin or Judah?

17 Based on בחורים shortened to חור(י)ם?

18 See *The Midrash on Psalms*, translated by W. G. Braude (Yale Univ. Press, 1959), pp. 53–6.

19 Babylonian Talmud, *Megillah* 12b.

NOTES TO CHAPTER 8 (pages 106–17)

1 See 'Ahab according to the Septuagint', *ZAW* 96 (1964), 269–79.

2 See 'Problems of text and midrash in the Third Book of Reigns', *Textus* VII (1969), pp. 20–1.

3 See 'The Septuagint's rival versions of Jeroboam's rise to power', *VT* 17 (1967), 173–89; and 'Problems of text...', *Textus* VII (1969), 11–13.

4 See 'The Septuagint's version of Solomon's misconduct', *VT* 15 (1965), 325–35; and 'Text-sequence and translation-revision in 3 Reigns IX, 10–X, 13', *VT* 19 (1969), 448–63.

5 See 'The Shimei duplicate and its satellite miscellanies in 3 Reigns II', *JSS* 13 (1968), pp. 90–1.

6 *Les Devanciers d'Aquila* (Leiden, 1963).

7 See 'The history of the Biblical text in the light of discoveries in the Judaean desert', *HTR* 57 (1964), 281–99; and 'The contribution of the Qumran discoveries to the study of the Biblical text', *Israel Exploration Journal* 16 (1966), 81–95.

8 *Chronology and recensional development in the Greek text of Kings* (Harvard University Press, 1968).

9 The fact that the Syriac, the noted hexaplaric witness, has Misc. 1 *sub obelo* is enough to show that Origen found Misc. 1 in his Greek *vorlage*.

10 See Shenkel, p. 63 (but Shenkel's reasons are not altogether beyond criticism; see *JTS* XXI [1970], p. 129, and also the criticism by E. Tov, *Revue Biblique* [LXXVI, 1969], pp. 430–1).

11 *Les Devanciers...*, p. 142.

12 *Chronology...*, p. 12.

13 One should note that ἀπαντήν (instead of ἀπάντησιν), which in 2: 8, 19 Barthélemy (p. 79) takes to be the work of the 'kaige' recension, occurs in 2: 35ⁿ in the manuscripts Ba₂ (though Barthélemy seems not to notice it). It could, perhaps, have entered the text of Ba₂ under the

influence of the occurrence in 2: 8, which is a duplicate passage. If Shenkel's criterion is reliable (p. 114, 2) the occurrence of ἀρχιστράτηγος in Misc. 2 v. h is evidence that Misc. 2 has not been influenced by the 'kaige' recension.

14 According to Epiphanius' fantastic account (*On Weights and Measures* 3–11), the 72 translators of the Pentateuch were shut up, two in a cell, each day from morn to eve.

15 *Textus* II (1964), 95–132.

16 See, e.g. Moses Hadas, *Aristeas to Philocrates* (New York, 1951), p. 73.

17 Sections 310–11.

18 See Jacoby, *Die Fragmente der griechischen Historiker* (1958), Dritter Teil, C, 722, 1–7 (pp. 666–71).

19 See Fragment 5.

20 Fragment 2.

21 See the interesting article by Ben Zion Wacholder, 'Biblical chronology in the Hellenistic World Chronicles', *HTR* 61 (1968), 451–81, and especially pp. 452–8.

22 In *Chronology and recensional development in the Greek text of Kings*. See also my review, *JTS* xx (1970), 118–31.

22ª The basic agreement which we noticed (p. 67) between the main Greek text and the MT of Chronicles against the MT of Kings may well mean, as F. M. Cross and his school would suggest, that both the Chronicler and the LXX translators were using what was basically a Palestinian text of Kings, whereas the MT of Kings may have been developed in Babylon. But the timetabling details, which have led to such a major re-ordering of the text, agree neither with the MT of Kings nor with the MT of Chronicles. They are, as far as we know, peculiar to the LXX, and certainly do not represent the original Hebrew. And the fact that the timetabling, which is such a prominent feature of 3 Reigns, is beyond all doubt secondary, as is the re-ordering of the text which it has occasioned (see p. 68), makes it quite likely that 3 Reigns' special chronology and its consequent re-ordering of the text are secondary as well.

23 If in the much debated phrase in *Aristeas* para. 30 the word σεσήμανται means, as G. Zuntz has cogently argued, 'written' or 'copied out', then Aristeas is explicitly referring to problems of 'text' (in the strict sense of the term) in the *Hebrew* Old Testament. See D. W. Gooding, 'Aristeas and Septuagint origins', *VT* 13 (1963), 358ff., and especially pp. 377–9 and the note to p. 377.

24 In his work *On Moses* 2. 25–44.

25 Section 302.

26 Section 307.

27 See, for example, his *Letter 71* (to Jerome).

INDEXES

SELECTIVE GENERAL INDEX

INDEX OF RABBINIC WORKS

INDEX OF MODERN AUTHORS